WORKING IT OUT

WORKING IT OUT

JOHN MASTERSON

MERCIER PRESS

MERCIER PRESS
Douglas Village, Cork
www.mercierpress.ie

Trade enquiries to COLUMBA MERCIER DISTRIBUTION,
55a Spruce Avenue, Stillorgan Industrial Park, Blackrock, Dublin

ISBN: 1 85635 447 4

10 9 8 7 6 5 4 3 2 1

Mercier Press receives financial assistance from
the Arts Council/An Chomhairle Ealaíon

Printed in Ireland by Colour Books Ltd.

Contents

Acknowledgments   9

Intro   11

1. Appetisers

Finding yourself … and where to begin looking   17
Don't lose your marbles   19
One small step   21
An independent life – no man is an island   23
Values and money   25
To see ourselves as others see us   27

2. Psychological Traps – Part of What We Are

It's just the way I am   31
Yes people … unable to say 'no' in any language   34
Are you an internet addict?   36
Regret – it goes in cycles   38
Your problem, not mine, thank you   40
Not guilty, your honour – but I did do it   42
Under pressure? So it a peers   44
Musterbation – it will drive you bonkers   46

3. Body and Mind – Logic and Psycho Logic

How is your samochuvstvie? A mind, body, spirit check   51
Talking to yourself – it is not the first sign   53
Must try harder   55
Count your blessings   57
Your daily mental workout   59
File it – in a black sack   61
Burnt out   63

4. The Rich Tapestry of Life

Early birds   67
Just a note to say thank you …   69

Sloppy versus neat – but don't judge a book by the cover   71
Keeping time – with different drummers   73
Age and experience – youth and passion   75
The Protestant work ethic – it's just an attitude   78
Perfect drivers   80
Service with a smile   82

5. Making an Impression

The words we use – I, me, mine   87
The gentle art of persuasion   89
The articulate mammal – or making a chump of yourself   91
Listen up!   93
Tone deaf   95

6. Confidence – The New God

Party animals   99
Shrinking violets   101
I can do that   103
Teachers for life   105
Best foot forward   107

7. Office Dynamics and Dynamic Offices

Your boss is half your age   111
Meetings … meetings … meetings … include me out   113
Many hands make light work – maybe, maybe not   115
Select the best for a winning team   117
The office ogres – control freaks and attention seekers   119
A bad attitude   121
Make a decision – any decision – please   123
Fighting and flirting – the Christmas party   125
Going offside? No, just emotional infidelity   127
Bullying – just say 'no'   129
A friend in need?   133
The right personality for the job   135
Losing the head   137
Office romance – tread carefully   139
Negotiate, don't fight   143
Timing is everything   145

8. Slings and Arrows

Giving out lemon drops	149
Rejected again – the power of SORRY	151
A gun to your head – take a walk	153
Stress – it's not all bad	155
Having a perspective	157
Anniversary 21 December 2003	159

9. Motivation and Getting Things Done

Praise – the oxygen of the office	163
It's exam time – read the question	167
Absenteeism – they've got the flu again!	169
Ambition – or why Paul McCartney still wants a No. 1	173
Brainstorming – the simple joy of knocking heads together	175
Procrastination – or one more cup of coffee	177
I've got a little list	179
Set your goals … some talk … some do it	181
New year resolutions	183
Get focused	185
PPPPPP	187
I've got an agenda	189
Hot groups	191
Learning	193

10. The Changing World of Work

Toys	197
Hooks of steel	199
Good work – if you can get it	201
Working mothers – now that's real work	203
I used to be a …	205
In love with your job	207
It's only a few envelopes	209
Homework	211
As good as your last job	213

11. Change – The Only Stability There Is

Routines and ruts	217
School for life	219

Taking the package   221
A new start   223

12. Recharge the Batteries

Feeling under the weather?   227
Jet lag – don't fly too high   230
Holidays – take your time   232

13. Thinking Outside the Box

Emotional leaders – Daniel Goleman   237
The lies we tell ourselves – Steve Chandler   240
Seeing with our brain – Ian Robertson   242

Outro

Television addict – in recovery   247
Conscious work, or automatic pilot   249
Quality of life   251
Jobless – but gainfully employed   253

Acknowledgments

This book would not have happened without my long-time friend, Mary O'Sullivan, who I worked with when we were both in RTÉ and am happily doing so again at the *Sunday Independent*. It was at her suggestion that I tried my hand at a weekly column that is vaguely psychological in nature and over the last few years gives me constant feedback as to whether or not I am hitting the mark. Her highest compliment is 'that was one of your parables'. Her harshest criticism is 'could you rewrite that by lunchtime please?' She has the sharpest of editorial minds and is always right!

My thanks also to Anne Harris who first gave me the opportunity to write in her pre-*Sunday Independent* days when she was editor of *Image* magazine. She has continued to be supportive. To editor Aengus Fanning for instantly saying 'yes, go for it' when asked for permission to use the title of my column for the book.

Thank you also to Madeleine Keane who over-saw many of these columns, and to John Chambers and Djinn Gallagher who ring and gently say 'this is what you wrote. Now I think what you are meaning to say is …' and with a deft word remove ambiguities and unintended insults. Any that have found their way back into this volume are my responsibility.

To my colleagues, Ros Falconer and Kevin Solon of Harmony, thank you for regularly supplying ideas.

To author Neville Thompson who regularly sends prodding e-mails and tells me to get on with it.

To my good friend, Brendan O'Carroll, for his wonderful motivational powers. He is one of a kind and I am just one of many to have benefited from his magic.

To my colleagues in Purcell Masterson in Kilkenny, John Purcell, Kevin Fitzsimons, Anne Ryder, Róisín Kinsella and Mary Tallent who put up with me going AWOL when there was business to attend to but a deadline looming.

Most particular appreciation to Mary Feehan, Mercier Press, who wrote to me suggesting a book based on the articles. We met, and to my astonishment, she had a file full of my cuttings which should have prompted a column on how to use flattery to get what you want from vain people. I did remark that I was glad she was a publisher and not a stalker!

To my sister Mag, brother-in-law Ted, and nieces Jade, Sarah and Tara I offer my sincere apologies for the occasions you have stumbled into print in a light you considered less than flattering. (Note to nieces – You are *not* on a percentage!)

Thanks beyond measure to Mary Kennedy, my harshest critic and most vigilant bullshit detector. My father regularly told me that as far as he was concerned I knew nothing about psychology and Mary has continued that tradition with style.

I get a pleasant dribble of letters from readers who have connected in some way with things I have written. These are always appreciated and thank you all.

Intro

I am a sucker for books with short chapters which probably says something about my attention span. But then George Bernard Shaw said that if anything was worth saying it could be said on a post-card. Our former Taoiseach, Albert Reynolds, received some stick for his 'one page' philosophy. I am an ardent Albert devotee in this regard. When it comes to speeches, I am consistent – less is more. So in this little volume I would far rather stand accused of not having given a topic the full comprehensive treatment than of having lulled you to sleep with detail. If the occasional sentence enables someone to look at things that matter anew, I will be well satisfied. In my time as an academic at Trinity College, Dublin I remember thinking how easy it was to get a core body of knowledge across to bright young students. But if you turned on just one or two people each year you felt you had really done your job properly. Then they went off and did it for themselves and probably enthused others in time.

I am not so much of a sucker for self-help books. I am a bit jaundiced with the notion that we must all be successful and have to strive to be better every waking hour. A world where everyone is socially skilled, in good humour, has straight teeth and is the correct weight to slip into their designer clothes and brightly coloured sports car seems unbelievably false (though I do like California!). I am also inclined to think that most of the solutions offered on the bookshelves are really expanded magazine articles, and would be much happier if they gave a good summary so that I didn't have to wade through the whole thing.

But I do know that people are finding the ordinary things that happen during our four score and however many years we have on this planet difficult at times. I know it because I am now a bit past half time in life (I hope, we know not the day nor the hour) and I have been around the block a few times. I have had the highs and lows, fallen in and out of love, felt great, felt lousy, felt energetic and felt exhausted, risen to challenges and gone down in flames, been accepted and been rejected. I have been lucky in my preparation for the rich tapestry of life. My parents were loving, caring and good fun. They made sure I got a good education, and coped with my hating the school I was in. They always supported me. These are great back ups in life. Like many children, I did not appreciate my parents fully when they were alive and there is nothing I can do about it now that they have passed on.

So it seems to me a good time to put a few thoughts down. When I was in my twenties, I was well versed in psychology and extremely naïve about life. In an early job as a young lecturer in Trinity College I remember teaching the standard differences between passivity, assertion and aggression in a social skills course and giving examples of how to ask a waiter for a different table in a restaurant. This at a time when I could scarcely afford my repayments let alone eat out in the Ireland of the 1980s. I would probably have equally blissfully doled out textbook advice on child discipline, workplace relationships, motivation for sports and jet lag. Now I know a little more, but more importantly have a great deal more faith in what other people know about their own lives and how they choose to live them. So in answer to the question 'what is a failure like me doing pontificating to others?' I would protest that 'failure' is putting it a bit strong and I hope not to pontificate, just prod.

I still feel lucky to approach much of life with the openness of a teenager. As I get older, I have less and less time for people who take themselves too seriously and have inherited my parent's bemusement at pompous asses. I become more and more conscious that life is not a rehearsal and that no one else is going to live it for you. It is up to you to knock as much craic out of our time here as possible, to leave the place a little better than we found it, and above all not to let the bastards grind us down.

So please dip in and enjoy. If anything in here makes some little change in how you go about your daily life and if that pleases you then I am more than happy. If not, go back to the beginning because you must have missed something! If you want to know how to have a perfect body, sociable personality, meet your ideal partner, have success at work and make your first million than read somebody else. If you are making a reasonable fist of life like the rest of us and every now and again try to make a change for the better then you will hopefully have a few thoughts provoked

For me going back over these thoughts of the last two years I came to one life-enhancing realisation. I am doing too much writing about golf and not enough playing. Meanwhile smell the flowers.

1
Appetisers

Finding yourself ... and where to begin looking

In the 1960s, everyone was trying to 'find themselves'. It was a new thing to look for and a real sign of social change that gave people some spare time on their hands. It was a psychological sign that we had entered an era of luxury, and perhaps self-indulgence. I remember using the phrase once to my father and meeting with, at best, a blank stare. Another man would have given me a clip on the ear. He came from that generation who just looked for a job, any job, and if they were lucky enough to get one they held on to it for dear life. Phrases like 'job satisfaction' would have seemed utterly pretentious to him. He sold insurance. It wasn't a very fulfilling or deeply meaningful way to spend your waking hours but you just got on with it. The real satisfaction was to be able to give his children the chances he had not enjoyed.

In two generations, we have become a land of opportunity not just in worklife but also in our social and leisure lives. We have become more demanding of satisfaction in all of these areas. And so we change jobs, relationships, friends and hobbies many times through life. Nowadays people can 'find themselves' a few times. Many discover they have a few selves in there – as The Edge said of Bono, 'He's an interesting bunch of guys'. Maybe there is more to you than meets the eye as well.

Some of these life changes may be very desirable. Others may be very painful. But in order to have control and choice over what we do we need to know ourselves as well as possible. Humans are the only animals with a capacity for self-reflection. Between eighteen months and two years, a child grasps the notion that they are a unique being. Some apes will recognise themselves in a mirror but other mammals do not. If you paint a red spot on a chimp's face he will see it in the mirror, realise he is looking at himself, and try to pick it off. Your family dog will just bark at himself as if it is another dog.

Back to humans. Try asking yourself some questions regularly to examine just who, or what, you are and find out if what you are doing is suited to your particular personality. Think about how you would describe yourself to someone at work, at a party, or on a foreign holiday. How do you present yourself in each of these situations and how do you feel about it? What are the things you do that make you feel satisfied, or proud? One thing should jump out at you. You probably have lots of different aspects of your personality depending on which situation you are in.

Yet, we all feel something unique and consistent about ourselves. You know you are still the same person that went gooey every time Gilbert O'Sullivan came on the radio. Or who couldn't understand how 'Please Release Me' kept The Beatles off the No. 1 spot for the first time. Older people feel a strong thread through their lives and in many ways do not feel very different from half a century earlier. But one interesting thing to emerge from studying how older people reminisce is that their memories peak around the late teens and early twenties, formative years, intense years, and 'finding yourself' years.

As we become more secure in our identities, we spend less time in self-reflection, that is, unless we are unhappy. So what can we learn about the self-indulgences of youth? Perhaps that it is not self-indulgence at all and that we should make an effort to think throughout life about the way we relate to our work, relationships and leisure pursuits. Then before dissatisfaction sets in we may be able to make small adjustments that prevent massively earth shattering ones happening later. Every time you hear yourself say 'I would love to ...' or 'I have always wanted to ...' listen up. Maybe even do something about it. It is probably a bit of the real you desperately trying to be heard.

The best way to think about how you relate to your work is to think about the things you actually do. To know yourself look at your behaviour. Do you like what you see? If not, which of the bits of you do you like best? Do they feel more like the real you? There is a lot of wisdom in the maxim 'be true to yourself'.

But remember – you have to find yourself first!

Don't lose your marbles

I received a thought-provoking letter from a Cork reader some time back and I thought people would find it interesting. Before long, it will probably pop up on an e-mail near you under the heading 'One Thousand Marbles'. It goes like this.

A ham radio enthusiast is fiddling away on the dial on Saturday morning when he happens upon a conversation between an elderly man passing on a few thoughts to a younger radio ham who he has never met. The young man has been going on about the familiar problems of balancing work and family and making ends meet and putting in the long hours and being exhausted when he does have time with his wife and children. The younger man is probably in his late 30s or early 40s, in that decade that can fly past leaving you wondering where it went.

'Well it took me until I was 57 to work out this small lesson', the older man said, and he began his story. One Saturday he did a little arithmetic and calculated that if the average person lives 75 years they have 3,900 Saturday mornings to enjoy. By the time he did this sum, he figured that he had already used up 2,900 of them and had 1,000 left, all going well. He headed down to a toy shop and bought a 1,000 marbles, one for every Saturday he had left, and put them in his den in a large glass jar. He began the routine of taking one out and throwing it away each Saturday morning. 'There is nothing like watching your time here on earth run out to help you get your priorities straight', he said, and as he signed off having made an impact on his younger work-frenzied listener and many eavesdroppers he said that he was going up to give his wife breakfast in bed and take her out for the day. But first, he was throwing out the last marble. He was 75 and with a 1,000 well enjoyed Saturdays behind him he was glad to have been granted some bonus time.

When I was studying psychology the big debate was about measuring behaviour and studying it scientifically. There had been decades of Freud and it was becoming clear that psychoanalysis was relieving people of large amounts of money without having much impact on their psychological problems. At the other end of the spectrum were those who argued that if you couldn't measure behaviour then there was no point in studying it. It was immediately pointed out that much of what contributes to what we do, goes on in our heads and cannot be readily observed by anyone except yourself. You don't have to tell anyone else the truth about what you are thinking. Indeed, you don't even have to tell yourself the truth about what is going on internally. But the big contribution Freud made was that he put human behaviour, feeling, emotions and thoughts firmly on the agenda as a proper subject to study and the basic point stuck – that our behaviour is not free and random. There are reasons why we behave and think like we do.

People still debate about the degree to which behaviour changes how we think, which it does – practise your driving and your confidence improves, and the degree to which thought changes how we behave, which also happens all the time. But often each of these can do with a little help which is what the marbles story captures wonderfully. It is easy to enjoy a well-spent Saturday morning and resolve to do it more often. Or you can decide that you are not bringing work home at weekends, and that will survive until the first work crisis and then family takes a back seat. But the marbles have a bigger meaning. They are a way to keep the behaviour and the thoughts going the same direction because they signify our time on this planet and remind us that it is up to ourselves to use that time well.

So I took out the calculator and wondered would I go greedy and add a few years! But thoughts of absent loved ones reminded me that the bonus days are here from the word go. Right now I am trying to keep myself going out for a run a few times a week. Maybe I will toss in a marble for every mile I run. I'll use 'bobblers' – the jar will look fuller!

One small step

We all have days when we get up, go from one cup of coffee to another, read a few trashy magazines, watch rubbish on television, maybe have a few drinks and go to bed having achieved absolutely nothing. They are totally wasted days, though in truth it is absolutely no harm at all to waste a day now and again. Provided it is only now and again. A few days like this in a row and it begins to become a habit – life satisfaction plummets as you begin to literally sleepwalk through life in a state of mild depression.

Often in those wasted days thoughts may turn to others who are more successful than we are. They are lucky. They got the breaks. They were born with the silver spoon and so on. Lucky them. Poor us. We ruminate about how we are just as bright, talented or whatever as they are. What we fail to look at in this mood is the effort they put in and the setbacks they had to deal with. Successful people fall over too, but they get back up and start all over again.

I am always intrigued by how big enterprises were once small enterprises. Denis O'Brien didn't start life with millions. But he built and built. The striking characteristic of people who keep building things is that they keep doing things. When you have a wasted day, not only do you do nothing, but you probably move backwards. You are doing nothing but the weeds are still growing. So the key to change is to do something. Do anything, but don't do nothing.

When you look back at any big change you usually see that it is made up of a series of small changes. Once you get it into your head to start doing small things then the habit of doing becomes ingrained and the rewards begin to flow. Often we are over-whelmed with the tasks ahead of us so we just give up. But if you spread out the steps then things look smaller. Anyone who goes for a walk by the seaside knows the experience of passing a house and talking about it. You keep walking and talking and looking back until the house has become a small speck. The small steps have become a mile. When I walk up a mountain I am always surprised by how soon the houses at sea level seem a long way away. When I put off painting a room for months it always intrigues me how by the time the first CD is finished the job is well under way. Each bit that is done doesn't have to be done again.

The credit card world has changed our attitude to saving money. This is a pity because saving up for something is a great way of seeing that small steps become big amounts. Nowadays we buy what we want and pay it off. Even children don't save up for a CD. They borrow the money from the parent and work it off. A generation ago, people would set aside £10 each week until there was enough to pay for the new carpet. Now the carpet might be nearly worn out before it is paid for. There is a huge psychological difference between an increasing balance in your deposit book and a decreasing balance on your credit card. It may sound old-fashioned but a move in the direction of saving up rather than paying off would do us all a lot of good. When Charlie McCreevy introduced the Special Savings Accounts he said that as a nation we had got out of the habit of saving and he was right.

Another big goal is to lose that stone that you would like to be rid of by Christmas. Well as it happens a stone is 14 pounds and Christmas is about 14 weeks away. A stone seems like a lot. A pound a week is easy. It is a walk instead of television, a little less drink without having to give it up, a few biscuits less without having to stop eating them. It doesn't even deserve the name of 'diet'. It is a small step each day, each week and a very satisfying result. The big benefit of small changes is that they stick. You are a changed person by Christmas and will not revert to the old you because the old you doesn't exist any more.

Someone described a goal as a dream with a deadline. Take five minutes each day to think about the small steps you are going to take that day and your dream has a much bigger chance of being a reality.

An independent life – no man is an island

Are you an independent person? Is it something you like in yourself? Or admire in others? Would it be something you would encourage in your children?

I had reason to ponder these questions recently. As part of a project I was involved in, I had the opportunity to complete a widely recognised, professional, personality assessment questionnaire. Now I will fill out anything in a magazine but this was the whole shebang administered by a psychologist. It took an hour, and it was the same form I had filled out as a student a generation ago. Being a hoarder, I still had the form from the earlier test. I wondered would there be any changes since the last time. 'I certainly hope so!' was the psychologist's immediate response.

This assessment compares you to your peer group over many characteristics but the one that jumped out was 'independence'. I was literally off the scale.

Now I have always been conscious of being independent. I was sent to boarding-school young and you had to stand on your own two feet. So I always regarded it as fairly normal to look after yourself, feed yourself, wash your own clothes, etc., and to take responsibility because if you lost your sweater it was your problem and you weren't going to get another one. All of these things would probably make me a dreadful father. But off the scale? That took me aback a bit.

While independent, I am enmeshed in social and loving relationships that I would be lost without. If any of them rejected me, I would be a helpless wreck in no time. Okay, I would pick myself up, but I wouldn't feel very independent.

We all perform various roles in life that make up part of who we feel we are. We all like to be a bit different, a bit of an individual, but most of us don't want to be all that much different. In fact, very different people usually make us feel a little nervous.

This prompted me to think back on the bread and butter

social psychology experiments dealing with just how independent people are. Many studies have looked at how people conform in the presence of others, do things that they think other people would approve of rather than what they want to do, respond to authority, and slip into and perform roles that feel comfortable.

Ask yourself this: when you are carrying out everyday things, do you think that you would behave in exactly the same way on your own as you would in the company of others? What if the others were friends, people you look up to, people you have little respect for, or people who employ you?

Think of the ways you like to stand out from the crowd and then think of the lengths you will go to to avoid looking different. We all know how a child can be upset if their clothes are different in some crucial way from other kids. But as adults, we also know the feeling of turning up over-dressed or under-dressed at a social occasion. Horror. Research shows that people are very influenced by the people around them.

And ask yourself this: if you were with a group of people who were all saying something that was different from what you could see in front of you with your own two eyes would you speak up and say so? You are probably confident that you would. But the answer for many people would more truthfully be 'no'.

Being independent and true to oneself is a bit of a contradiction because we all take account of the situation we are in – even the most independent people. If you didn't you would rapidly appear freakish.

Sitting at a computer thinking to yourself is probably one of those independent things that are supposedly 'the real me'. It does not always feel that way. In fact, sometimes it makes you feel a bit dependent and needy. I think I will go and look for a hug! Or talk to the dog.

Values and Money

'He just doesn't seem to have an ounce of ambition', a mother said to me of her teenage son. To me he seemed to have plenty of ambition and like many teenagers it bordered on fantasy as he strummed a guitar for hours with images of limos, wealth and probably groupies swimming around his head. He just didn't have what his mother saw as ambition – namely lots of points in the leaving cert and a respectable job.

It struck me, though I kept my mouth shut, that the man she was married to didn't have much ambition either. He was in one of those jobs where you progress up the ladder, and he had gone up most rungs but not to the top, by turning up every day and not rocking the boat.

Some people are not so much lacking in ambition but very much determined by the need to avoid failure and so they try to avoid situations where failure is possible. They can usually be found in jobs where there are no clear measures of performance and where promotion is largely based on time in the job. As someone said the person who aims at nothing is sure to hit it. But work is not everything and people who plod along at work may have ambitions outside the workplace, or may indeed harbour notions of a better life for their children. They may well have begun their working life when opportunities were a great deal more limited than today.

We need some ambition to make things happen, to do something rather than just talk about it. But can it become the very thing that drives us to lose any sense of perspective about the values we use in our lives? We get what we want and then we are caught between wanting more and being terrified we will lose what gains we have made. What the 'Jones' have may become more important to us than what we really want ourselves.

But what do you want? Ambitions are tied up with values, and values are often linked to status. Men tend to be more status conscious than women and this can be seen in the drive they attach to work. It can sometimes push all other aspects of life to one side,

25

and lead to a total lack of respect for those who have chosen a different path. At the post-rugby-match drinks anyone who said that they were on the look-out for a six-year-old VW because they thought buying a new car was insane in the city would be seen as contaminated and encouraged to drink up rapidly before they infected anyone else!

Now and again it is no harm to step off the status and ambition ladder in our own culture and widen the perspective a bit. Having just spent a week seeing how the other half lived in Central America, I found myself thinking today about the ambitions and values of many of the people I met working there – the lawyer who worked on the side of land disputes and doesn't earn the big fees, the programme director who could run a multi-national with all the perks but chooses to run a 'multi national' with no profits, and the doctor who gave up the six figure salary that goes with high-tech medicine to set up simple hygiene programmes that save a lot more lives.

Yes, these were three ambitious people. Each had targets. Each knows what they want to achieve. They are achievement-oriented doers and each would tell you that without ambition there would be no progress.

They are not saints. I am sure they have their bad days just like the rest of us and end up apologising profusely for things they said and did in the heat of the moment. But they have given thought to what they wanted to do with their time and it brought with it an energy that comes from ambition that fitted well with their particular personalities and values.

I don't know what that 'idle, good for nothing teenager' strumming his guitar will end up doing. But I have a hunch he will make his parents proud. If they are smart enough to let him be.

To see ourselves as others see us

Wad some Power the giftie gie us,
To see oursels as ithers see us!
It would frae monie blunder free us.

Robert Burns – 'To a Louse'

Are you ever completely taken aback by how people describe you? I don't just mean behind your back. I mean to your face. It may be an unexpected compliment. Something is being discussed and the person beside you suggests you do 'x' because you are the sort of reliable person who always gets things done. 'Who? Me?' is flashing through your brain. Is that what they think of me? I always thought I was seen as a bit erratic, but with a certain flair and style.

Or worse, a piece of sensitivity is called for and you are ruled out because it is well known that you will go in with feet first and leave collateral damage all over the place. In your own mind you are a model of diplomacy and tact. But that is not how you are seen.

There is a maxim in psychology that the meaning of something is the result it produces, and not the result that was intended. So, if you tell someone that they are looking fabulous, and their response is 'so you thought I was overweight the last time we met' it doesn't matter one jot that that thought had never entered your head. What matters is that it was uppermost in the listener's head. And that is what the compliment turned out to be. An insult!

We all know this to some degree and we pick our words more carefully with people who might be a bit touchy. But we still get it wildly wrong at times. Remembering that we are dealing with another person with his or her own personal baggage and tailoring what we say is an important part of successful communication. But while we focus on the other person and the message we want to get across, we frequently forget about the other important side of the equation – the way they see us.

So just how well do you know yourself? How accurate is your self-image? How well do you know and anticipate the reactions you produced in other people? Are you frequently misunderstood?

To do this requires thinking about ourselves and that is an area where a little can go a long way. A well-adjusted person doesn't think about himself or herself all that often, probably less than 10% of the time. If it is more often than that, it is usually because the person is unhappy, or even depressed.

We also think of ourselves because of the situation we are in. Walk into a roomful of strangers and anyone will become self-conscious. Sometimes this type of private self-consciousness can lead to anxiety and awkward behaviour. But also the more useful 'public' self-consciousness comes into play. We are sensitive to the way we are perceived by other people. We are concerned about how they see us. Do they like us? Do they see us as friendly? It matters to us that they think a bit like us, that they share opinions that are important to us.

To be sufficiently self-conscious that you are aware of what you are doing without increasing anxiety levels, and at the same time to be aware of the way others are seeing you and the results of your behaviour, are important social skills for anyone who wants to have a positive impact on those around them. These skills are the very essence of diplomacy and the bread and butter of the way politicians operate.

At work, politics isn't all about promises and telling people what they want to hear. You have to deal with your co-workers day in, day out and not just in four years' time.

No, politics in the workplace is about knowing what you want to happen, watching the results of your actions, taking into account the way others are seeing you, and adjusting accordingly.

To succeed you need to pay a little more attention to yourself. But only a little. You are really not thinking of yourself at all. Think of it as thinking of other people. It sounds better!

2

Psychological Traps –
Part of What We Are

It's just the way I am

'I can't help it. It is just the way I am'. How often have you heard people use that excuse to explain something that they have just done, or not done? The picture they present of themselves is as if they believe they have absolutely no control over their behaviour because they are stuck with a personality that drives them in one particular direction and that direction only. The next thing they will be telling you is that it is a family trait, that they took after their father or mother. The implication is that with two generations to consider the cement is set even harder. This is the perfect excuse not to change. 'No one in our family was ever any good at singing'. Well, that puts paid to the karaoke night!

Then there is the first cousin of 'just the way I am' which is 'that's the way we've always done it'. How often have you heard that at work and at home? At least it allows in some chink of light by implying that change would be possible but that it has been firmly rejected.

When you hear any of these phrases be on the look-out for frozen thinking and behaviour that is stuck in a rut. Now I grant you that there are times when the very same thought processes can be positive as in 'the Kellys always know how to make the best of a situation and enjoy themselves'. But most times, you hear the 'the way I am' mantra – a self-limiting and handicapping phrase that is bringing the person down. It is not a life-enhancing phrase. It is a psychological straitjacket.

We may not have any choice over whether we will be six foot two or five foot five, gay or straight, bass or baritone. But we have an enormous amount of choice about how we choose to feel about it. Our emotional responses are the result of how we think about a situation and not the situation itself. Too many people do not act as if they have that ability to change.

People often handicap themselves so that they won't have to deal with failure. They don't apply for the job so there is no chance of rejection. They don't talk to the girl they fancy and then have to watch when she is thrilled that someone else pays her some attention. A very successful attractive woman I met at a conference was delighted to be included in a dinner invitation. She had spent the last three nights watching television in her hotel room. Everyone had assumed she was bound to be occupied and did not risk a refusal.

Two people look at a situation. One sees a situation fraught with problems and threats. Another sees a golden opportunity. Which one gets up off their posterior? Which one is more likely to feel good?

Anyone who has played a sport knows how important your thinking and attitude is to performance. The golf handicap is a good motivator because your handicap is based on the best rounds you have completed. When your performance improves, you have the handicap there to remind you of your level. But any golfer will tell you that they can go out on the course and say to themselves that they won't do very well because they haven't played much recently. Rest assured they won't get any surprises. They have given themselves the excuse to play badly and they will live down to it. Now it may well be that they have had a hard few weeks and are quite happy to just enjoy the fresh air without any pressure on themselves. But the point is the same. How you think has a huge influence on what happens.

It is a good exercise to take out a piece of paper and write down a list of things that you believe about yourself. Look at all aspects of your life. What sort of person are you in relationships? How do you deal with your children? How do you approach problems? What parts of you are like your parents? Which are different? What is your typical mood like and does it change through the day, week or time of year? Do you take care of your appearance? Are you healthy?

Take a little time to think of the picture of yourself and then consider whether there are some things on that list that you would like to change. If so, what you are going to do about it? If you hear yourself saying 'that is just the way I am' look yourself square in the face to see if you are using it as an excuse for doing nothing.

The alternative, a small helping of personal growth each day, is a much better recipe for an enjoyable and fulfilling time on earth.

Yes people ... unable to say 'no' in any language

I think it was Dorothy Parker who said of a particular woman, well actually not a very particular woman, that she could speak nine languages but was unable to say 'no' in any of them. It is one of those put downs that you wish you had thought of first.

Leaving aside matters of virtue for the moment, we have all worked with people who say 'yes' to everything, but deliver very little, and leave debris in their wake. They make promises but just don't keep them. They treat deadlines as if they didn't exist and will have a million seemingly reasonable excuses and explanations, lots of which involve saying 'yes' to still more people who will in the fullness of time be let down as well. It can affect home life when saying 'yes' involves staying late to get everything done, and then cancelling what had already been arranged with family or spouse, who are scratching their heads with exasperation wondering why it is always their partner who takes on the extra work?

So just why are some people 'yes' people and what can you do about it?

There are three reasons, and with patience you can do something about them. One is that some people are very concerned about getting on with other people and think that not offering to help will lower them in the eyes of the other person. Secondly, they have a very poor ability to look ahead and see the consequences of agreeing to do a particular task on their work and home life. Thirdly, once they have undertaken to do something they are just hopeless at organising themselves to get it done in time. The good news is that while you cannot do a lot about someone's need for approval, once you recognise that it is at the source of the problem you can do something about the other two parts of the problem.

The key to change is to remember that the source of the 'yes' person's trouble is that they have a strong focus on people. There is no point in taking them to task directly and giving them a hard time because they will say whatever you want to hear to get you to stop. That will include more promises which will not be kept and by that stage the relationship is bound to be deteriorating. This may be someone you are stuck with so you better work with what you have got. They didn't deliberately set out to let you down. They probably feel terrible, but they just don't feel all that responsible and do not have the skills to stop repeating these failures.

First and foremost, they have to feel it is safe to talk to you and that talk should be kept honest between the two of you. One of the things they will have to learn is that there are many options they could have taken along the way which they did not see as options. Right from the beginning, they could have explained what they had on their plate and why they could not undertake the additional work. At the next stage they could have avoided taking on new things coming up to your deadline. Or they could simply have discussed it and got some help. Prioritising is not their strong point.

You are dealing with people who try to please others so the negative consequences should be explained in terms of their effect on the people they work with, not on something abstract like profit, or other people they do not know or care about.

Finally, you need to get a deeper level of commitment from the person. Simple things, like asking them to summarise what is involved, help enormously. Writing the steps down can be even better. You are letting them experience that a decision has real meaning if it is agreed between the two of you. Including points at which progress will be assessed greatly increases the chances of success. These people are often the most loyal people you can have on your team so it is worth putting in the effort.

Alternatively, you can do none of these things and let them drive you mad.

Are you an internet addict?

Q: How do you know you are addicted to the internet?
A: When you go to the bathroom in the middle of the night and check your e-mail before going back to bed.

You may well laugh. But the internet seems to be as effective as a one-armed bandit in keeping human beings staring at a screen. This is beginning to have consequences for people who are neglecting the real world, and for large companies where employees are spending vast amounts of unproductive time on the net. This was the technology that was supposed to make people more efficient! One American study found large numbers of people spending up to 40 hours a week on the net. And a university found that most of their first year drop-outs had been doing all night sessions at the computer but they weren't studying!

The slot machine gives you back enough money to reward you for your effort. At times, you will even get ahead. You might think about quitting and putting the money in your bank account. But you probably won't. As you go on the pay-outs become thinner, but they are just enough to keep you in there. Eventually you stop because you have run out of money. All fine if it was an innocent flutter and you had decided to stop once your budget was gone. But we have all heard of people whose lives were ruined by the inability to stop.

The internet has a similar quality in that your efforts are constantly rewarded. You get replies to your e-mails. Now that broadband is becoming popular, all those frustrating waits for the information to download are gone. You find out things. You discover new and interesting sites. You congratulate yourself on how proficient you have become.

But most of the heavy users get particularly hooked when they are interacting with other people from the anonymity of their own home. Post a message on a newsgroup and soon you will get replies from everywhere. Join a group about a hobby or a medical problem and people from all over the world share their experiences. Then for the real step into a virtual world there are the MUDs, or Multiuser Dungeons (they began in the days of *Dungeons & Dragons*) and MUSHes (Multiuser Shared Hallucinations) where people spend time in the most elaborate of fantasy worlds and games, each with their own community ethos.

Anonymity is one of the important attractions. People can interact in a world where looks do not matter. Soon webcams will put an end to it (would you interact with someone who would not let you see what they look like?), but for a time the less beautiful in the world have a medium that works. Physical appearances play a dominant part in our daily lives. We disproportionately attribute all sorts of positive qualities to good-looking people. They are seen as more intelligent, their jokes are funnier, we listen more intently to them, and so on.

Now one can, via anonymity, get as much attention as Pierce Brosnan and Julia Roberts combined. People try out different parts of their personality, aided by the disinhibiting effects of privacy. They can express ideas that they are afraid are stupid and it doesn't matter if they are. They share their thoughts with others and friendships are formed, some with far more intensity than real life.

Whether it is pseudo friendship, virtual games that never end, or just surfing for the best value holiday on the planet more and more people are spending time at their computer terminals. Once 24-hour flat rates become standard this will increase and before long it will be commonplace for companies to monitor office internet use, not so much because of what employees are looking at, but because of how much time they are spending at it! This will be a hot workplace issue. People do not like being monitored. But it will be essential.

The final test – do you have more friends on the net than in real life? It might just be time to do more off-line living.

Regret - it goes in cycles

'Not a night goes by I don't dream of wandering through the house that might have been a home'. It is a Dixie Chicks' song from 'Home' about life – if she had made a different decision. You can feel like this even if you have made the right decision and would do so again if in the same place. There are very few occasions when option A is all good and option B is all bad. If there were, a good handful of us would still grasp option B firmly. No, most times, there are good and bad things about the several options open to us and we have to make a choice. You have to decide to move to a new job you really want, but it entails moving from a house that you love and seeing less of friends you enjoy. How wonderful it must be to be able to face eternity with the words '*je ne regret rien*'. In real life most of us clock up unhappiness about choices we have made over the years and look back thinking 'if only' without realising that mistakes are part of what we are. Being perfect is not.

That is all very fine if we reminisce with a bemused air wondering what would have happened if we had moved to Tokyo, of if we had married Thelma which was on the cards but the timing was all wrong but anyway life with Louise is very happy, thank you. But sometimes people can become so consumed with looking back at what might have been that they become stuck in the past – about which they can do nothing. Someone quipped that it is hard to drive a car if you only look in the rear view mirror. Middle age in particular is a time when people take stock of their lives and may not be very satisfied with what they find. Then they do dumb things like search out their teenage girlfriend on the net as if they hadn't done any living in the intervening 30 years. The result? More emotional mayhem usually.

The things we regret fall into a number of categories and if we are more conscious of them we can lessen the chances of sadness when too much water has passed under the bridge. You need to get into a mindset of knowing that there are always both good and bad consequences of choices and that this is a part of life.

People look at their job situation and rarely regret taking too many chances, risks and opportunities. No, they regret still being stuck in the same place. Some people take a risk early, it doesn't work out, and they become frozen because of the fear of encountering that regret again. In my first job, I remember making a substantial error of judgement and assumed I would be fired. A considerate boss took me aside and told me that the only people who didn't make mistakes were the ones doing nothing and to stop brooding and get on with it. The world wasn't going to end.

People look at the balances they have achieved between work, family, children, friends, hobbies, interests and themselves and any of us who faces that list honestly can still decide to change and pay more attention to one or other area.

To move on you have to make peace with the results of decisions you have made in the past. If you had to deal with the same issues with your life experience, would you still do the same thing? Today you may be able to go some way towards making up for the losses that resulted from some of the choices. The next-door neighbours you left a decade ago still have a phone. You may have the money now to visit places you missed when you opted for the burden of a mortgage instead. You can still mend that relationship. Or let it go.

Some time back I came to the realisation that if I did not buy a motorbike I was going to regret it at some stage. So I bought one and have got endless enjoyment from it apart from the practical benefits of getting around town in about a quarter of the time. I have no regrets. I do however have some disappointment. I have learned that several leather-clad women of my acquaintance regard this clothing as a fashion item rather than protective gear for a pillion passenger. They show marked reluctance to feel the wind on their faces and the freedom of the highway. I am convinced that in years to come they will experience some regret on this score. But then no one is perfect!

Your problem, not mine, thank you

About 25 years ago the concept of co-dependency began to be very popular in the alcoholism and drug abuse fields. The central idea was simple. Someone had a problem and by caring for them, you not only supported their problem but also became part of the problem. Further, you then became dependent on being a caring person, a bit of a martyr, and got your satisfaction from fulfilling other people's needs. Gradually you lost all sense of self and, because of someone else's problem, you ended up with a whopper of a problem yourself.

That was all very fine but so plausible was the idea that self-help books began to apply the concept everywhere and parents, children, lovers, spouses of anyone with any problem whatsoever were seen as likely candidates for developing co-dependent traits. The term began to be used to refer to any person involved in a dysfunctional family who has experienced a chronic loss of self. The co-dependent person looks at life as defined by other people and becomes unaware of their own needs and how to satisfy them. It is sometimes spoken of as 'relationship addiction' because such people often get into relationships that are one-sided, emotionally destructive and abusive without being necessarily physically so.

While the idea has been stretched beyond breaking point, a central truth is worth keeping in mind in all of your relationships. When someone behaves in a way that causes you to do something you do not want to do you have choices to make. It may be someone at work who screams and roars and everyone placates them. It may be a control freak spouse who sulks if you go out with friends. It may be the person who turns on the tears whenever they want to be the centre of attention.

People gain control of other people incrementally. Each time they go a little further and gradually you are trained to their needs and your own needs have become secondary. It is not unusual to hear people who have been in such relationships complain that they find it very hard to feel any real sense of self, so powerful has been the focus on other peoples' demands. Typically their self-esteem has been eroded and characteristically they tend to do more than their share all of the time, be hurt when people don't recognise their efforts, feel guilty when they assert themselves, feel a strong need for approval and recognition, have difficulty in identifying their own feelings and making decisions confidently. We can recognise the alcoholic or drug addict but we are less adept at spotting the bully and controlling personality. Every time we let someone away with bad behaviour, we chip away a little bit of our personality and self-esteem. Key questions to ask yourself are – Do you keep quiet to avoid arguments? Are you always worried what others think of you? Have you ever lived or worked with someone who belittled you? Do you feel like a bad person when you make a mistake? Are you uncomfortable expressing your true feelings? Do you have difficulties with intimacy?

One of the downsides of co-dependence becoming fashionable was that it tended to give caring a bad name. The very act of compromising one's needs to help a loved one was deemed a symptom of a psychological disorder and that is total nonsense. If your child is having problems with drink or drugs or whatever, it is a normal human response to give them all of your attention. Empathy is good for you and so is caring. Friendships which last are usually based on mutual caring and occasional self-sacrifice. These feelings are based on the important desire to make the lives of those we are intimate with, happier. So, treat the myriad of 'self-help' books with a pinch of salt at times.

In short, it is your life and you have to decide to what extent you want others to mess it up. To do that you have to make the distinction between normal loving caring which forms the warm fabric of life up and down the country, and wasting your good deeds on people who need to, and are well able to, sort out their own messes.

Not guilty, your honour – but I did do it

Nobody is perfect. We all make mistakes. We all do things we are a bit ashamed of. A normal reaction is to feel guilty about our behaviour. But how much guilt is enough? Too little and we run the danger of becoming almost amoral in our dealings with people. Too much and you are stuck in a rut, beating yourself up, and probably depressed as well.

Early life experience has a big influence on how you feel about yourself when things that you had a part in go wrong. People who have endured constant criticism are prone to think badly of themselves and to strive for perfection to escape criticism. Their efforts to be perfect are bound to fail thus perpetuating the negative feelings they have about themselves. Some people are blamed by other people for how they feel – 'it is your fault that I am feeling like this … you are doing this to me, etc.' – and as a result may end up always trying to make others happy and enduring guilt when they don't or can't, which is most of the time.

Religion is often at the root of guilty feelings about oneself, and usually that may not be a bad thing. But as religious belief changes some of its strictures may still have a grip. The person who intellectually feels that it is fine to have sex outside marriage may still be tortured by guilt if they have had a strong family history of being told how to think and feel about sexual matters.

If you are stuck in a guilt trip, the first thing to do is to re-examine the situation that is troubling you and hopefully you can gain a better perspective on your behaviour. People are inclined to blame themselves for things that other people, or situational factors beyond their control, had a big role in bringing about. So take a situation you feel bad about and put it to a simple test. You may have lost your cool with someone at work and regret it. Or you may have kissed one of your spouse's friends at a party and are mortified, embarrassed, terrified someone will find out and you want to turn the clock back. You may just be feeling bad about not making time to visit someone in hospital. Or about the white lie you told to avoid going to a boring party. Perhaps it is the scratch you put on some other shopper's car at the supermarket.

First of all, go back to your intentions before the event happened. Did you fully intend things to turn out as they did? Did you see it as a possibility? Or maybe it never even entered your head. Pick a figure between one and ten to signify how much you fully knew what you were doing and how it would end up.

If another person is upset, who is responsible? Is it 100% your fault? Maybe the other person should take some of the blame. Again, pick a number and build up the perspective picture.

Think about what other factors may have contributed to the situation. Maybe they were badly parked. Was it such an old banger that they wouldn't notice, or a gleaming new BMW that you knew was going to cost a fortune for a little scratch? Again, try to identify and evaluate those other factors and ask do they lessen the responsibility and guilt you are placing on yourself.

When people feel guilty, they may only see the negative factors. But it is very unusual for a situation to be all bad. There are usually pluses and minuses. Try to step outside your circumstances and assess what percentage of the situation is good and what percentage is bad. You may be surprised at what you find.

I am not for one moment suggesting that all guilt is bad and that a guilt-free world would be a wonderful place. It is important that we keep a connection between our behaviour and our emotions. We spend a great deal of time teaching children the difference between right and wrong and it is vital for all of our well-being that most people agree in general about how to behave in society. But values change, life is not black and white, or simple, and throughout life people find themselves with dilemmas for which there are no easy answers – and doing things that do not sit easily with their moral code. But that does not make them bad people. Recognising the full complexity of human life may help you get out from under the burden of guilt, while still going through life making a good attempt at separating right from wrong and taking the better road.

Just one small point. If it is my car, please leave a note.

Under pressure? So it a peers

I heard a story about a very happy couple, living a full life, in good health and both in their 90s. Over dinner, they were asked what it felt like to have reached this stage of life. She looked at him and it was clear that they had an answer worked out for this oft-repeated question. 'One of the nicest things,' she said with an impish smile, 'is that there is hardly any peer pressure these days!'

We hear a lot about peer pressure in the adolescent years. We worry about teenagers drinking more than they should, or younger than they should, and blame 'peer pressure'. A lot of time and energy is invested in training children to be able to make their own decisions without being over-influenced by the group mentality. It is a difficult time in life because young adolescents are particularly concerned about fitting in. As well as wanting to do what others do there is the more complex problem of wanting to do what you believe others are doing. There is a stage when they dread the 'are you a virgin?' question and many will embark on more sexual activity than they are comfortable with in the mistaken belief that everyone else is doing it.

But peer pressure does not leave the scene as we become adults. We read of the sensational accounts of cult mass suicides when a group can bolster each other in a crazy belief before embarking on mass lunacy. At a more mundane level, large parts of industry function effectively because of peer pressure. High-tech industries, in particular, are peopled by competitive employees who care how they are viewed by their co-workers and one of the effects of this is that they need little or no supervision. They will work just as hard without it because they want to be seen to be up there with the best. Indeed a good manager may have most difficulty in getting them to take a bit of a break and recharge their batteries now and again.

Mark Twain did not have much respect for our ability to be individuals when he wryly observed that we are 'discreet sheep. We wait to see how the drove is going and then go with the drove'. Have you ever found yourself behaving that way? If you say 'no' I think you are probably lying to yourself. Think about this. Do you ever feel pressured to do what others are doing? How do you deal with it?

Fashion is a good example. Advertising gradually changes what is acceptable to wear so that we buy clothes long before the ones we have wear out. It doesn't matter how immune you are to trends, virtually everyone is familiar with the feeling of not wanting to be seen dead in what was once your favourite attire. It applies to cars, phones, where we go on holidays, which restaurants we eat in, the couch in the living-room … There is that day when it just looks wrong and we feel the pressure to change.

Much of our behaviour in the workplace is influenced by what our peers think and what we believe they think. Employers are increasingly aware of it. Investing time in creating a pride in the company and its work will reap handsome rewards for any employer. And it will have an impact on negative things such as absenteeism. Pulling a sickie feels very different if you feel you are letting your team down rather than some faceless corporate identity.

Health, and how much we are responsible for our own health, has become a big issue in the US where employers look at how an increasingly overweight workforce is affecting the success of the business. How can they get people to take better care of themselves? A programme to enhance gentle peer pressure is one route they take.

We feel like individuals but we are part of a group most of the time. To have maximum control over doing what you want to do for yourself at work and at play you need to listen carefully to yourself to find out why you are doing what you do. Is it for you or for them, or do the two happily coincide?

If you think you have gone a long way away from the pressures of adolescence, you are fooling yourself. There are just more of them and they are subtler.

Musterbation - it will drive you bonkers

Have you ever wondered why you feel the way you do when something untoward is said to you? In everyday life we are often criticised for things we say or do. Criticism is often expressed clumsily. A label is used. You are told you are 'lazy' or maybe 'stupid'. How do you deal with criticism? Do you just shrug it off, accept it and decide to do something about it, or does it prey on your mind incessantly?

It is not what happens to us that is upsetting, but our view of it. We don't even need another person to make us miserable. There are plenty of opportunities for DIY misery. Take the following. You have some visitors coming to the house and you want everything just right. Ninety-nine per cent of the preparations are made but you have forgotten to do one important thing. There are no flowers in the hall. You forget how much you have done and proceed to beat yourself up over the bit you failed to do. And once that word 'fail' rears its ugly head, you are only a gnat away from calling yourself a 'failure'.

One person is down in the dumps. Another couldn't care less. The difference is in how different people view the same events. A key to how we feel about things is to look at the type of rules that we apply to ourselves. Sometime we are far too all-or-nothing in our thinking. If it isn't a total success, it is a total failure. See if you are one of those people who thinks that you 'should' do things or 'must' do things. These two words are first cousins and guilt follows each of them as surely as ice cream and chips end up on your thighs!

Psychologist Albert Ellis was so aware of the power of the word 'must' that he coined the term 'musterbaters' for people whose lives are dominated by the word. Some people deeply hold beliefs like –

I must be competent....
I must not leave myself open to criticism ...

I must be liked by people …
Other people must treat me fairly …
My life must be pleasant …

If you 'must' be something, you have no room to move. You are set up for failure so the consequences of not doing something that must be done perfectly are that you are a total failure. The result of not being liked by your neighbours is that you think you are a rotten person and do not deserve to be liked. The downward spiral that results from putting these huge strictures on yourself are guilt, anxiety and depression.

Of course, it is completely irrational to hold beliefs like those above. But we all do hold some beliefs about ourselves that are irrational, or at least unreasonable. Lots of people believe that they need to be loved in order to be happy. Or that they need to be successful to be happy. Or that they must never make a mistake. In order to find these beliefs and de-programme yourself a useful method is to catch yourself thinking 'should' and 'must' and see how reasonable they sound.

I should/must brush my teeth each night won't do any harm. I should/must always be nice to people no matter how they treat me is more questionable. I should/must never make a mistake is clearly bonkers and will drive you that way.

If you think someone dislikes you, and follow on that you are not a likeable person, rest assured that you become less likeable immediately and increase the chances of people not liking you. You will prove yourself right, but at what cost!

If you think you must do something, try asking yourself 'what if I didn't?' The chances are the consequences would not be all that drastic and you will have got a monkey off your back!

3

Body and Mind – logic and psycho logic

How is your samochuvstvie? A mind, body, spirit check

There are various times in the year when we are filled with good intentions. New Year, milestone birthdays, travelling abroad, or just having a good long weekend. Most good intentions remain just that but if you want to look back on the next 12 months with pride, maybe even as a year with some turning points, then here is a small nugget of advice. Keep an eye on you *samochuvstvie*.

No. I hadn't heard of it until recently either. I came across it in a book written by a Russian high altitude climber called Anatoli Boukreev. His job was to get less experienced climbers to the top of high mountains. As they prepared for a summit assault under difficult conditions, he would always mentally assess the *samochuvstvie* of his clients.

Samochuvstvie means something like an impression of a person's state of being, the combined and observable aspects of a person's mental, physical and emotional state. Once you start to think of a person, most particularly yourself, in these terms you will be surprised at how useful the concept is. This one word focuses us on how inter-related the various aspects of our existence are. Just as years ago people thought of intelligence and personality as two separate aspects of a person and now see how much they over-lap, so we are becoming more and more familiar with the way different aspects of our life are best understood in conjunction with other parts of ourselves.

Recently I heard some people using the greeting 'How are you in your mind, body and spirit?' I must admit that this has something of a tree-hugging feel to me, a tincture of religion, and comes from that touchy-feely area that I would happily see confined to California. But as I listened to the phrase, it gradually dawned on me that it is a very useful trilogy to keep in our minds each day. It is a bit like golf. The days when the driving is straight, the approach shots are confident, and the putts roll in are the ones you want more of.

But while the golfer will isolate the part of the game that stinks and get a lesson, how many of us will give similar attention to our mind, body or spirit? Not enough of us.

Body first. Anybody who doesn't take exercise these days must have a desire to enter the next world more rapidly then necessary. Even a good strenuous walk has effect on your *samochuvstvie*. You feel stronger, think clearer and if you keep at it the emotional high of going in one notch on your belt is little short of winning the Lotto. How often should you take some exercise? Every day.

We give our bodies a hard time. In particular, we pour too much alcohol into them. We don't put them to bed early enough, and all too often we have to get up too early after a lousy night's sleep. When was the last time you woke up fully relaxed and refreshed? If you have difficulty remembering then do something about it. I write this in my post-Christmas rehab period – that is the first morning after a good mountain walk and a full day with not a drop passing anybody's lips! The holiday period has done its job. I am feeling whole again!

Which brings me to emotions which I like better than spirit. Sleeping like a log is a good indicator that the emotions are at ease with each other. But we all have periods of nagging doubts, every-day worries or guilty feelings which play havoc with our outlook on life. Sometime things as simple as a walk and easing off at the dinner table will be sufficient to get life's woes in perspective. Other times we need to talk.

To make an occasional check on your mind, body and spirit might be the most useful resolution you make for the coming year. It is not rocket science and just a little shift in outlook may result in a big jump in your satisfaction with life.

Wishing you all good *samochuvstvie* for the foreseeable future.

Talking to yourself - it is not the first sign

Who do you talk to most every day? Your children? Husband or wife? People at work? Who is the most important person you talk to every day? Well the answer to both questions is … yourself and it is not the first sign of madness!

Imagine you are going into a crowded room where you don't know very many people. What are you saying to yourself? Is it something like 'I'm really looking forward to meeting someone new'? Or 'I wish I had worn the other jacket'? Or maybe, 'I hope Mick is here and I will make a bee line for him'?

Somebody at work pays you a compliment. Are you thinking, 'I'm glad they noticed. It was worth the trouble'? Or 'I'm glad it was Jean who said that because she knows what she is talking about'? Or perhaps, 'I wonder what they want'? We are constantly communicating with ourselves. It is as if we are giving a running commentary.

We interpret situations and, to a degree, we act accordingly. But when we are talking to ourselves perhaps we are not always saying the most useful things to ourselves. Maybe it is worth having a listen now and again to see if there are any consistent patterns that could do with a remould. Sometimes the running commentary can get a bit biased. The glass can be half empty or half full. In the most extreme case a person can be constantly driving themselves into depression or anxiety with inappropriate self-instructions but that it not what I am talking about here.

We interpret differently because we are different. Any teacher will tell you that the same event is interpreted differently through the class. 'Now stay quiet unless you have something worthwhile to say' makes one child feel worthless while another might think that the teacher wouldn't know something worthwhile if it sat up and bit him.

Think of the five-foot left to right putt on the first green. Are you thinking 'I always miss these' or maybe 'I'll nudge it up and it will probably go in but I won't leave myself a three footer back' or even 'nice and steady and I can't miss'? Three different styles, and each style will then respond differently if the putt goes in, or if it does indeed miss. There are people who practically reject the positive: 'I was just lucky. I probably won't get another putt all day'.

There are a number of thought patterns that are worth looking out for. We all have bits of them. Do you see things in black and white so that if everything isn't perfect you see yourself as a total failure? One negative makes a disaster. Everyone has an enjoyable meal but the cook cannot get his or her mind off the one vegetable that wasn't quite right.

Some people go around with the idea that everyone should love them, and spend their entire lives in contortions trying to please people. Obviously impossible, but people get caught up in it.

Then there are people who think that everything in life must be under control, and get very upset when it is not. In extremes, we see the control freak, but there are plenty of steps along the way.

Do you find yourself saying 'I should' very often to yourself? Have a think about it. It is a great way to feel guilty.

If you make a mistake are you thinking of it as something everybody does and you will get it right next time, or is your inner-self telling you that you are stupid?

How we habitually think is often evident in what we pass on to our children. An eight year old gets nine out of ten on a spelling test. One parent praises. The other asks which one they got wrong. Witness 'the sins of the father' being passed on to the children – and the virtues too.

So, have a think about how you talk to yourself because the ripples go a long way. Remember, everyone interprets things differently. So some of you reading this are already saying that it is a load of balderdash, while others are deciding to put a notebook in their pocket and write down a few patterns. I am sure there is somebody having a good think about the number of times they have pointed out that their children are the untidiest they have ever seen and why can't they be more like the Murphy's who are the very epitome of perfection.

Think about it.

Must try harder

Some days you look at the pile of work facing you and just do not know where to begin. Worse still, you don't want to begin at all! You would rather be in bed, in town shopping, even doing the ironing, or in the garden. Anywhere else. You look around and see other people cheerfully getting on with things. But you know that you haven't an ounce of get up and go in you. 'What is wrong with me?' you think. You feel lousy about yourself.

All the self-help books tell you to start with the most difficult task and the others will then seem easy. Right now, you would rather walk on hot coals than face that particular chore. The magazine article beside the bed tells you how much better you will feel after a brisk 30-minute walk. 'Go take a hike – an ice cream would make me feel better', your barely functioning brain chips in.

Your conscience is telling you that you must try harder. You are letting the others down. We all have seen school reports that say 'must try harder' and this creates the notion that there is some mystical effort quality out there that will solve everything. Ask yourself did you ever go back to school the next term all fired up with enthusiasm because the maths teacher gave you a 'must try harder'.

You are waiting for the electrician to come and do a few jobs. You finally get him on the phone and he says 'I've a lot on this week but I'll try and get to you by Friday'. What do you expect to happen?

One friend tells you they are going *to try* to give up smoking. Another tells you they *are going* to give up smoking. There is a world of a difference between the two sentences and you know well which one is more likely to succeed.

We get things done when we stop the trying and just get on with the doing. I know this. I have known this for many years. Yet, today I was caught red-handed. A colleague phoned and asked me for some work that I had been putting off. 'I'll try and get it done by next Wednesday,' I replied and if it had been on television, they could have put 'lie' on the screen. But she was wise to me and got me to give a firm commitment. What I was really saying was come back to me next week and I will have a new excuse.

In the meantime, we all give ourselves a hard time because we feel we are not trying hard enough. The result is that we feel bad about ourselves and our energy and motivation goes even lower.

So, take this in. It is not unusual to feel over-loaded. Everyone feels it now and again. The problem is not just about managing time. It is about managing yourself – if you are berating yourself and feeling guilty then you are being a bad manager of yourself.

To work well you need to feel good, not bad, about yourself. A common trait among successful people is that they spoil themselves. Regularly. They end up with lots of achievement and lots of spoiling. One positive feeds the other positive and instead of a downward spiral where life is hardly worth living there is an upward one with opportunities for work and fun all over the place. Which life would you rather live?

So I will do that chore that I have been putting off. But first, I think I'll take nine holes on the golf course. Why? Because I deserve it. I'll knock off that other little chore in an hour or two this afternoon. Life is so much more enjoyable when you feel a little whistle coming on!

Count your blessings

The attitude with which you approach life has a big influence on what you get from life. If you have a sunny disposition you are going to have more enjoyment than if you approach everything from a cantankerous viewpoint. We can all spot the difference between someone who smells the roses and the one who only sees the weeds. We know who we would rather share company with!

I was at a Saturday morning family football game in the United States recently. It was a relaxed morning with parents and friends shouting encouragement to the ten and eleven year olds. To say it was mixed ability is an understatement but the organisers made sure that everybody got to kick the ball now and again. At the end, the teacher got the children into a huddle. I assumed this was the team motivational talk. No. The children each bowed their heads and thanked God for the chance to play soccer on this lovely morning and then ran off 30 seconds later to get on with Saturday.

I was rooted to the spot and probably initially outraged. We hear about religious maniac suicide bombers from other cultures every day and here we are bringing up another generation with the mindset to take them on rather than try to understand each other. Then I chilled out a little. I am not a religious person but like most Irish people my age, I was educated in a school where religion was central to everything. Before every meal, we had a moment of silence and thanked God for the food. It struck me forcibly on that sunny Carolina morning that something fast disappearing from everyday life is a disposition of gratitude for the life we are living. The pendulum has switched to complaint, dissatisfaction and wanting more and more. It is really a miserable style of thinking with which to spend our waking hours.

In today's compo culture the shopper who trips in a shop does not get up thinking how glad they are not to be hurt, but more likely how much will they get for it. The person in the restaurant doesn't marvel at the amazing array of foods available but on what they wanted that is not on the menu. If you are over 40 think of the foods regularly eaten in Ireland today that you had never seen or even heard of in childhood. The list is long.

There are occasions when we are thankful and say so. Usually it is when something bad happens to somebody else. You hear of the friend who loses their job, the person who is ill, or you attend a funeral that is taking place many many years too early. 'It puts it all in perspective', we say to each other with people barely admitting the fear they have that it could have been them. We count our blessings and we do it all too rarely.

I had forgotten that 'Count Your Blessing' was a hymn until I hit a site on the internet that plays it as soon as you click. The sentiments give pause for thought:

When upon life's billows you are tempest tossed
When you are discouraged, thinking all is lost
Count your many blessings, name them one by one
And it will surprise you what the Lord hath done.

When you are only thinking of the things you lack and that could be better, you are in the world with an experience of 'wanting' and 'dissatisfaction'. When you look around you, or go back though your diary and see the things you have done with an attitude of gratitude the world seems a more comfortable place. This doesn't have to turn you into a smiling fool. You will still strive to do all sorts of things, but with a different outlook. It certainly hasn't stopped me wanting a BMW Z4, but it is a bit less urgent.

When Johnson Oatman Jr wrote the words and Edwin O. Excell set them to music over a hundred years ago the world was a less material place. But the fundamental psychological problems of living were much the same:

Are you ever burdened with a load of care?
Does the cross seem heavy you are called to bear?
Count your many blessings, every doubt will fly
And you will keep singing as the days go by.

Your daily mental workout

There are few things as frustrating as having something on the tip of your tongue and not being able to remember it. It could be the name of someone you met yesterday. It might be a film you saw, or a place you spent a weekend. But try as you might it just won't come. Then you forget about it and, hey presto, out of nowhere it pops into your mind. As often as not at 4 am when you could comfortably do without it.

As you get older, it happens more often. In your 30s, you console yourself that there is just so much going on that you cannot remember everything. You start to write things down. Your filofax, or these days Palm pilot or XDA, comes into its own. Once it is written down, it gets done. Then there are the things that you forget to write down, and lo and behold, they aren't done.

There are some things we simply don't forget. Have you ever met a smoker who couldn't remember the brand they smoked? Or someone who just cannot recall what it was they wanted a pint of, or what was the mixer you put in gin? Some people would forget their partner's name quicker!

Now we are well used to our bodies becoming less reliable over time. We all know the simple steps to take to keep them from going to seed. But mostly they remember what they are supposed to do. The legs may get slower, but the left foot remembers to go ahead of the right and we get from A to B without falling flat on our face, or having to stop and wait for inspiration as to which leg goes next. But our bodies only remember to do the things that we keep on doing. I was somewhat taken aback when I went back to riding a motorbike after a 20-year break that a lot of muscles had to do a crash course in relearning. Swinging one's leg over the bike with a confident nonchalance is one of those skills that goes rusty without practice.

So is it the same with our brains and what can we do about it? Can we do any mental gymnastics for our memory? Are our mental muscles ready to benefit from a little refresher course?

Well, yes, they can be given a workout. Many years ago, I wrote down a few notes from a newspaper article about how to keep your brain young and fit. This must have been in my 30s because it was that stage in life that everything ended up in my filofax. Sadly that is also the stage when I cannot for the life of me remember whose idea these exercises were and I offer them my apology. But I have found them useful over the years and you might like to enter them in your laptop, or stick them to the fridge with a magnet from your last holiday. That is, the holiday that you have trouble remembering!

This will take you about 10 minutes in the morning. Now 10 minutes in the morning is a lot and I let this discipline slip regularly. But I promise you if you stick with it the benefits compare to regular games of Boggle, Scrabble and chess.

Firstly, sit down comfortably, and count backwards from one hundred to zero as fast as you can. That will get you warmed up.

Next, go through the alphabet at full speed, and for each letter come up with a word that begins with that letter. It goes like this … ashtray, banana, car, dungarees … do it as fast as you can all the way to Z. It is not as easy as you might think.

Now think of 20 men's names, counting them as you go. One, Paddy, two, John, three, Seamus, four Dan and on until you have 20. Easy? Try it and don't use the same names every day.

Now 10 names of places. Do Ireland one day, the world the next. Countries one day, towns another day.

Finally pick a different letter of the alphabet each day and think of 20 words beginning with that letter as fast as you can – door, dove, dingo, drum, double … until you have 20.

You've got the idea and you may just feel the benefits. Mess around with the tasks to your heart's content. Instead of places think of 20 rivers, films, or songs. Do men's names one day, women's the next. First names one day, surnames the next.

It will only take 10 minutes, and I ask myself why it is that I so rarely find time to do it! Maybe you will be more successful. Best of luck.

File it - in a black sack

Ringo Starr, in a philosophical mood, was talking years ago about how the success of the Beatles had changed his life and that it was not all good. He reckoned he now had more than a thousand LPs in the house. Very nice you would have thought at the time. He then compared himself to one of his good childhood friends in Liverpool whose limited means had bought him about 25 treasured LPs. He knew every note on every one of them. He knew the words. Each had been chosen with care. Each was highly valued. For Ringo the problem had already become not knowing what to play and being so swamped he wasn't sure what he liked, loved or valued any more.

The problems of a superstar Beatle have now become the problems of every one of us. It is not unusual for a house to have several hundred CDs. There could be a hundred in a teenager's bedroom. I was browsing last week and came across the Kinks' Greatest Hits at a good price. I hadn't heard any of those Ray Davies' songs for years so I bought it. I discovered that night that I already had two copies of it that I had totally forgotten about – and there are plenty more like me!

Few tasks are more thankless for a parent than getting a child to tidy up their room. Being some way organised has a purpose because the state of the bedroom in childhood has a good chance of being the state of the office in later life. When I was a child, it was relatively easy to tidy up my room. It is not rocket science to keep 7 LPs, 20 singles, 30 books, birds' eggs, an autograph book, back issues of the *New Musical Express* and *Golf Monthly*, and my photographs under control. You could fit it all in one of those under the bed storage boxes they have now and have room left over. But crucially everything I had was crammed with meaning for me. If there was a fire, I could have written out a fully accurate inventory if I still believed life was worth living. So could Ringo's friend.

Today's bedrooms are probably smaller than a generation ago but they are cluttered with possessions so numerous that you would have to plan a route to get to the bed. This clutter is reflected throughout our home and work lives and quite simply our brains are not designed to cope with so much information. The more we have the more we cease to relate in a meaningful way to our surroundings. My father used to have a theory that it was only a matter of time before the entire world was buried under photographs. Everyone is entitled to their special photographs, but the point he was making was that vast amounts of what we accumulate is just junk. Junk has to be dealt with and it saps our energy for dealing effectively with work, home, people and life.

I am not for a moment saying that people have to be obsessively neat. Neatness can be a 'disease' that takes up more energy than junk. Nor am I advocating a Feng Shui approach to life which always strikes me as just a load of nonsense to sell coffee table books (i.e., more junk) … when I start to read about the 'smooth flow of chi through space' I have no difficulty in finding the dustbin. But what I am saying is that we can only deal meaningfully with a certain amount of information. I know my desk is littered with various projects at times and every now and again, it becomes a huge burden. The solution is always to take an hour and decide which things are never going to go anywhere and file them in the black sack. If they are not staring at me, I never have to think of them. It is the work equivalent of going through the wardrobe and throwing out everything you haven't worn for a year. You won't wear it next year either.

I knew I had too much rubbish when I stopped writing my name on books. So, take a section of your life and be ruthless. You will be delighted to find that the technique will begin to apply to your diary. You will stop arranging things you don't really want to do. You will begin to have the time and enthusiasm to enjoy the things you want to do. It always strikes me just how good successful people are at managing time. It is because they know better than most that it will not stretch so it matters what you do with it.

So, go through your life with a black sack. Do it soon before they begin to weigh the bins!

Burnt out

Do you ever notice yourself going to work on a Monday and thinking about the weekend? I don't mean the one you are just finishing. I mean the next one. Pause for thought because it is one of the early signs of job burnout.

Are you inclined to be irritable? Do you feel tired all the time? Your sex life has become, well, if not perfunctory, you are certainly not keeping the neighbours awake. Maybe you have caught yourself grinding your teeth. You are lowering your standards in the office and doing just enough to get by. Your concentration is dreadful, and you are forgetting things that make you wonder is senility setting in early. Yep. They are all signs and you had better do something about it.

Over the years, I have caught myself slipping into it more than once and now I know my signs. Yours may be different but there is a fair degree of overlap between us human beings. For me the first thing I notice is getting exasperated with people. I have certainly reached the stage of thinking they are stupid, but usually keep that to myself. Not that it isn't written all over may face. Then I find myself driving with my jaw clenched, and around that time I notice I haven't had a good belly laugh for a while. In fact, nothing bothers me much, good or bad.

Spotting the build up is half the battle. Then it is time to learn from the cat. Yes, the cat. Cats, by and large, are very healthy psychologically. Now the cat that I know best is permanently curious and never bored. She moves from task to task as she wishes, hunts birds with complete failure and remains optimistic, approaches everything playfully, eats sparingly, gets plenty of affection and shuns it when she has had enough and always has a good night's sleep. Oh and she is a non-smoker.

Burnout was first recognised in the caring professions where over time the emotional toll built up and people saw that a break was necessary. These were also jobs where people loved their work and were inclined to give their all. That can be a problem in many areas. You may love your job, but if you don't keep an eye on it, you will be so consumed by it that you will end up hating it. Is your job the main focus of your life? If so, then no matter how much it fulfils you today you are on the road to burnout.

For some people it is just the sheer volume of work that grinds them down. Do you stay late in the office? Well, start leaving the same time as the others. First one day a week, then two and so on. Don't bring work home with you because that just means you never leave work. If it is that vital, finish it first. But it probably isn't and will be done better tomorrow.

Perhaps the most disturbing aspect of burnout is that one becomes cynical about work. Cynicism is notoriously hard to reverse, and is usually accompanied by a very negative and low self-image – and it can spread like a virus.

From the employer's perspective it is worth monitoring if the person's workload is genuinely manageable, and that the person feels a good degree of control over how they carry it out. Beyond that, recognition of effort is vital to keep people vital.

If burnout goes on too long the psychological effects will turn into physical problems. Oh and by the way, the graveyards are full of people who were absolutely indispensable at work. So, I have my plot booked, but I am in no rush.

4

The Rich Tapestry of Life

Early birds

There is a part of the day that large numbers of people scarcely realise exists. It is worth making the effort to become acquainted with it. I am talking about the dawn and the hours immediately after it when the animals begin to stir and far too many humans are still in the land of nod, unaware of what they are missing.

For some people the very idea of getting up hours before they have to fills them with horror. Teenagers are particularly bad at rising early but it is becoming clear that there are good biological reasons for this and it is not just because of staying up too late watching television. Canadian research suggests that adolescent body clocks are out of synch with the adult world and that their natural waking up time is between 9 am and 10 am. Some American schools have taken this seriously and are now beginning the school day later to coincide better with when the pupils are at their peak of alertness and receptiveness. Researchers said some students were literally sleepwalking through the day. One school noticed significant improvements in the educational performance of its students. I can hear a howl of 'I told you so' coming from teenagers the world over!

For adults going to work this is a luxury rarely on offer. But as luck would have it around the onset of middle age humans tend to move to becoming more 'morning' type of people. The entire world of work, however, is structured as if we were all 'morning' people firing on all cylinders between 9 am and 5 pm.

To find out whether you are more naturally a morning or an evening type ask yourself a number of simple questions and see if a pattern appears. If you had absolutely no commitments tomorrow what time would you choose to go to bed at? If you have to do an hour of concentrated brain work what time of the day suits you best? If you have to dig the garden, do you prefer morning, afternoon or evening? If you have a very late night what happens the next morning? Do you wake up as normal, or wake up and doze, or sleep an extra few hours?

Our bodies have a 24-hour rhythm but we all differ and it is worth finding out what time of day suits us best for the work and leisure we want to fit in. If you are a morning type, your body temperature will peak much earlier in the day. Evening types tend to be very grouchy in the morning and take a while before entering fully into the spirit of life. There appears to be a genetic reason controlling what part of the spectrum you fall on.

Which brings me back to the pleasure I get by getting up very early in the morning. Apart from the things you see and hear – I saw a mink and a stoat last week – there are practical results. There is the benefit of no phones or people. I know of one senior lawyer who swears that the work he gets done between seven and nine is worth a whole afternoon and consequently feels no guilt about a long lunch and a browse in the shops.

But it may not be all good. The early bird may catch the worm, but they may be more stressed as a result. One English study showed that early risers have higher levels of cortisol, the body's main stress hormone, and that the levels remained high all day. Further they found that in a ten-week follow-up study early risers reported more muscle aches, cold symptoms and headaches and significantly worse moods. Someone said that while the early bird catches the worm it is the second mouse that gets to eat the cheese! Think about it.

Perhaps it is a case of moderation in all things because I found the complete opposite when getting up between five and six two or three mornings a week. It is easy to get a lot done at a leisurely pace and that in itself produces a sense of well-being.

Try it once on a sunny day and see how you fare. If you bite the head off everyone you meet that day than maybe take it that you are more of an evening type!

Just a note to say thank you ...

If praise is the oxygen that gives people energy, then saying 'thank you' comes a close second. Like many good manners, it is a habit worth cultivating.

Many of us remember being sat down a few days after Christmas and told that the thank-you letters had to be written before New Year's Day. We may have got a few days' extension, but it had to be done when there were far more enjoyable things to do. So, we ticked off our lists of aunts and uncles and marked off which ones needed different letters because they would show them to the others and they couldn't look identical. Few of us realised that in this small childish task were contained all the ingredients for properly letting people know that we appreciated what they had done. If this lesson was learned well it would stand to you.

Some years ago, I was back and forward to London covering the story of the end of the Margaret Thatcher era. It was a media circus with everyone scrambling to find the right interviewees to explain what was going on and in these endeavours, I was lucky to be working with Olivia O'Leary. After a particularly frantic programme on a Tuesday night, we headed back to Dublin unaware that we would be back in London into the fray again on Friday and Friday was the day when everyone we wanted to talk to was on their way out of London. Phone call after phone call drew blanks. Until I found one prominent man about to leave his desk and head for the country. He hesitated.

'I'll do it. I'll be with you in an hour. I got such a nice letter from Olivia last time I couldn't let her down'.

I didn't ever see that letter. But I know thought and effort went into it. It was appreciated.

How often have you smouldered at work because your effort was not remarked upon? Or do you remember occasions when the wrong person was thanked for the work? It certainly sets the emotions rumbling.

Put the shoe on the other foot. Were there times recently when you have failed to acknowledge the contribution one of your colleagues made?

What then are the crucial rules for thanking people? You don't have to think any further than what you did those days after Christmas.

Firstly, sooner is better than later – and you avoid that apology you find yourself muttering the next time you bump into the person.

Then you should thank the right person or people. Sometimes it takes a little effort to figure out just who did what. It makes a big difference to get that right. It shows that the appreciation is genuine and not just automatic. People are very sensitive about being left out. They are also sensitive about people who step forward to claim credit that is not rightfully theirs.

Thirdly, get it in proportion. There is no point in going on and on about something which people feel is part of their job anyhow. There is even evidence that too much recognition of normal work will diminish performance. Likewise, there are some degrees of effort that deserve more than a cursory 'thank you'.

Finally, be sincere. There are those who 'say it with flowers' at the drop of a hat and it means little or nothing consequently. Sometimes it really is the thought that counts and not the size of the gesture.

So whether it is a postcard, phone call, flowers or e-mail you should probably be doing more of it. You will feel the better for it. If you want to be mercenary, it will probably even pay off in the long run!

Sloppy versus neat – but don't judge a book by the cover

You are in a dreadful rush and stop in to get your newspaper on the way to work. You have the exact change in your hand. In front of you is this person who first of all cannot decide what to buy and then changes their mind about three times. You are about to blow a gasket when they finally get their choices made and are told that that will cost €4.97. Then the saga begins of the creature in front of you going through every pocket trying to make up the exact amount with twos and fives and ones instead of just putting down a €5 note and getting it finished.

Based on what you have just seen you are probably making several other assumptions about how that person will behave in other situations. You might expect them to be a poor timekeeper. You most likely assume that their desk at work is a mess, and that they are forever losing things.

The message is simple. When we watch a person behave, we make guesses about what type of person they are and how they will behave in other situations. If you reverse the two people in the shop above what would our 'slob' think about the person with the exact change. Well what would you think?

Probably that they ran their house with military precision, put their clothes on hangars before going to bed, washed the car on Saturdays at 11.30 and wouldn't allow a cigarette or sweet papers in it on pain of death. Everything is put in the diary with very neat handwriting. The word boring might also come to mind!

People hold strong beliefs about how and why other people behave the way they do. Usually we make these judgements based on too little information. Take our two people in the shop.

Some people are just not good at planning and organising and it is a feature of their life and that is just the way they are. It is not something they have any great choice about.

Other people may adopt that type of behaviour as a style. They are literally thumbing their nose at what other people think.

They may have the idea that only dull, boring people are well organised and that truly creative people (like themselves) are not organised in trivial ways because they are on a higher plane. They consciously adopt an airy-fairy exotic persona as their image. For such people the notion that the person behind in the queue is fuming is a bonus, and will only encourage them to take things a bit slower.

Or it may be that the person is typically very well organised but a particular stress or bad news has completely disrupted them. We have all seen people who literally go to pieces when a loved one is ill. I clearly remember a very competent colleague being completely unable to concentrate on anything for a day because the cat was going to the vet for an operation!

And the organised person in the shop? Some such people are completely confident and self-assured and that is the way they go through life and that is it. This type of person tends to like an orderly life, but does not get unduly upset if things go a bit awry.

Others exhibit the same behaviour but from a different perspective. They are very anxious people with a deep need for a predictable, orderly, controlled environment around them. Spill a cup of coffee on the carpet and you will know which is which!

In short, some caution is always advised when deciding you know the key to someone's personality. A little knowledge can be a very misleading thing.

Keeping time - with different drummers

I spent a glorious summer in Albuquerque, New Mexico, in the days before the filofax had really taken off and time management had become a religion. I attended a summer school and each day consisted of a morning session from 9.30 am to 12.30 pm and an afternoon session from 2 pm to 5 pm. Except for the courses given by the Navajo Indians who merely put morning and afternoon on the notice board. The westerners went ballistic. 'But what time should I turn up?' they screamed to be met with a gently reply, 'in the morning and we will start when we are ready'.

So what happened? People arrived at the Navajo courses in dribs and drabs from 9.30 am on and chatted amiably about anything and everything. Usually around 9.45 am, the lecturer asked was everybody ready to begin and productive work ensued until everyone felt like stopping, oddly enough usually not far from 12.30 pm. Then they had an enjoyable relaxed lunch secure in the knowledge that a good morning's work had been done.

In the other rooms at 9.30 am people were glowering at their watches. The lecturer would start and then two people would come in late and disrupt everything. A sarcastic comment about punctuality would follow. Then he would go back over the last point and three more very apologetic late people would have to climb across chairs and by the time the whole affair got started you could cut the tension with a knife. They were counting the minutes from 12 to 12.30 pm.

How often do you find that you do not allocate enough time to complete a meeting and end up at home that night feeling frustrated that so little was achieved? Do you finish meetings on the hour without giving sufficient thought as to what is to be achieved in the time and how many people need to contribute? The Hungarians have a nice system where meetings begin at seven minutes past the hour. So, people arrive in dribs and drabs and have a sociable chat and most times all are ready for the task in hand at seven minutes past. The tradition began with the Opera giving patrons that few minutes grace before commencing the performance.

For contrast, picture the following. You have meetings in your diary on the hour at 9, 10, 11 and 12. The 11 am is just a five minute drive away. The others are at base. In the car on your way to work you feel the stress levels go up because two of those meetings are to complete unfinished overdue business and you wonder will today be better.

At 9 am, only three of the eight people needed are there. The rest arrive complaining of traffic within 15 minutes. You settle down, a mobile rings, and seven people listen while one person takes the call. Two people have to leave at 9.50 am and you promise to e-mail them about the outcome of the meeting.

Your 10 am is not much better and you have to leave early for 11 am and can't find a parking space. By lunchtime, you have spent four hours working and achieved virtually nothing.

Time to think like a Navajo. Think of the task and who will be there. It is important that the relevant people are present and not people whose input will be minimal because when someone is there you can rest assured they will want to say something. It may add nothing but it will still take time, time that could be better spent by that person and by your group. So set aside enough time for everyone to have his or her say and for a decision that will stick when arrived at and arrange the occasional five minute break for people to check their mobiles.

My guess is that you will go home that night with a number of things accomplished and put to bed in a manner that will not require revisiting and going over the same old ground at the next meeting. Work would be a lot better if the diary forgot about the hours and just said morning, afternoon and evening and had a little box for you to tick if you got something worthwhile done.

Age and experience - youth and passion

I never expected to be 50. It is not that I expected to have died by then, but that it seemed so impossibly far away. But then I never expected Mick Jagger to be 60. Or Bob Dylan to release a great album in 2002. Wouldn't you think that they would grow up? Things are getting serious when Cliff Richard is showing a few lines.

I have never paid much attention to age. Until I was 20 or so, I was always one of the youngest at everything. Then comes the surprise that someone you are working with is five years younger. Gradually more and more people are younger and fewer are older. Then you reach that day that most of them are half your age. But it still never bothered me much.

Probably because of the significance of the half-century, two things caught my attention recently. The first was a few lines from Tom Paine, a man who had a significant impact on the American constitution. He published *The Rights of Man* in 1792 and there lurking in the middle of it are a few lines about being 50. He wrote: 'At 50 though the mental faculties of man are in full vigour and his judgement better than at any preceding date, the bodily powers for laborious life are on the decline. He cannot bear the same quantity of fatigue as at an earlier period.'

Then I came across several studies showing that some managers hold negative stereotypes of older workers. They are seen as being less adaptable, performing less well, and less capable of dealing with new technology. On the plus side, they are seen as more stable, reliable and honest.

Now this did not seem like most of the 50 year olds I know, the bulk of whom maintain a workload that would leave younger people falling by the wayside. Most of them are productive, often because they have to produce the work to keep younger people in jobs. They are still hungry, if not for money, for respect and success. These people have a lot of experience at their fingertips. So, both Mr Paine and the managers cited in the studies seem to be missing the point. Or are they?

The more I thought about this the more I came back to two fundamental issues – the personality of the worker, and the work they do. People who enjoy getting things done constantly get that feeling of having achieved something, and the major difference as they get older (within limits) is that they have more resources to bring to the task. The person with the most alternatives is the most powerful in many situations, and if you can combine experience with flexibility the chances of success are good.

The other factor appears to be the nature of the work they do. None of the people that came to mind had routine jobs. Each day presented new problems and opportunities, and while there was a structure to life, there was great variation within that structure. So no two days are the same for the farmer, journalist, craftsman, photographer, architect, chef, builder or the man who bends the car back into shape after a shunt in the traffic.

Combine the right attitude with the right job and the negative effects of age get pushed away. Combine that attitude with the wrong job and the job will win. Combine a dull person with a dull job and it seems crazy to put the blame on age for their lack lustre performance.

Largely the people with the right attitude on my list were in the private sector. In many instances, they were as good as their last job so they stayed good. They were in situations where they couldn't get away with taking it easy and collecting a pay cheque until they were 65.

This brought me to the difficult task faced by that group of people who have to deal with benchmarking. To compare the private and public sectors must be one of the most difficult tasks they have faced, as the gap in understanding between the two groups is enormous. They are a different type of people in fundamentally different work environments. As different as chalk and cheese.

It strikes me that if you are looking at performance, attitude to work and productivity, age is one of the last places to look for expectations.

Absolutely Fabulous hit the nail on the head when one of the characters had to go into therapy to face the big four O. Last winter I was signing up for an hour on a go-cart track and amongst the details you have to fill in is your age. I filled in five zero and one of the teenagers in the party pointed out that it really should be five one. I have only just finished my 50 therapy. It should be everyone's privilege to lie about his or her age. Anyway, none of this hurt half as much as being passed out by the young pup when I was flat out on the straight!

The Protestant work ethic – it's just an attitude

What sort of attitude do you bring with you to work? Are you one of those people who counts the minutes until you are free again? Or do you always stay late? Maybe bring some files home with you? Once you have started, do you have to get it finished? I met a young author recently and asked her how she managed to get time to finish her book with so many other work commitments. 'I'm a completion junkie', she told me.

I would lay money that this doesn't only apply to her worklife. If she decides to wash the kitchen floor, I am sure you could eat off it when she is finished. If she is climbing Croagh Patrick, she won't stop half way. If she sweeps the floor none of the dust is pushed under the rug. For all I know if she parties she is last to leave the nightclub.

Then it dawned on me. This woman was committed to working. She set herself high standards. She persevered when times got tough. She was the living embodiment of what sociologists call the Protestant Work Ethic. That she was not a Protestant matters not a jot! The term came into use in different times, around the turn of the last century.

Psychologists have devised many scales to measure the attitudes with which people approach their work. They talk about work involvement and use it to explain why someone who hasn't an ounce of commitment at work will move heaven and earth on behalf of the local hurling team. Or how the person who shows no initiative from nine to five demonstrates the organisational ability of a military commander when making a surprise party happen.

They also examine people's need for power, and need for achievement, but one of the most enduring concepts in describing behaviour in the workplace has been the Protestant Work Ethic. It is usually seen as being made up of several behaviours. Foremost is the belief in the importance of hard work. There is a high premium on being rational rather than emotional in how one approaches problems, and there is an abhorrence of waste. Laziness is seen as a big sin, and the pleasures of the flesh are treated with great suspicion, and best kept under control. When you put it all together 'all work and no play makes Jack a dull boy' comes quickly to mind!

Maybe the above is a bit of a caricature and the whole package doesn't come in the one person. But many people have some of these behaviours. I am beginning to blush as I remember lighting fires in my childhood days. Nothing as extravagant as a match was used. Firelighters wouldn't have been let in the front door. No. Instead, newspapers and old letters were torn and folded into 'spills' which sat in a mug on the mantelpiece and were used to light everything from cigarettes to bonfires. It has been a hard habit to break, and I still feel guilty lighting a firelighter. Even worse, using a match to do it!

Look around and you will find people who save carefully, don't waste things, and always seem to be on the go. These are high on PWE measures and it all goes back to childhood where a few simple standards of upbringing lay the foundations.

Such children are encouraged to make their own decisions and that fosters independence. They are taught to delay rewards until they have done what is required to earn them. They learn to manage their emotions and not be enslaved by them. Finally, they are required to finish what they began before enjoying a sense of pride in what they have achieved.

This young woman became a completion junkie, got a huge advance, and has a smile from ear to ear. Maybe the PWE has something to recommend it after all!

Perfect drivers

Every now and then, we begin a criticism with the words 'It's nothing personal …' The next word is bound to be 'but', and I for one flinch when I hear the phrase. Because it *is* personal and it is about to hurt. There are some criticisms we can absorb easier than others, and there are some areas of life that feel more personal than others. Oddly one of the touchiest areas where we all take it personally is driving. Why? Because we all believe firmly that we are good drivers. Try a little test. On a scale of one to ten where one is a learner driver and ten is a fully competent driver with no room for improvement where would you put yourself?

I had three interesting car experiences recently which made me think about how well we are trained to drive. I lent a car to my sister and she managed to run out of petrol. This means that she didn't see the warning light for 100 miles. She probably didn't even look at the instrument panel. I hasten to add that I find her a safe, careful driver. She has passed driving tests at the first attempt in three countries and has never had an accident.

A woman friend borrowed the same car having heard the above story. She wondered if the car used any petrol at all because it seemed to be permanently stuck on half full. On day two she realised that she was looking at the temperature gauge.

Before this sounds like a 'women drivers' piece let me add that I found I was blocked in on coming out of a restaurant recently. My female colleague said that I had room to squeeze out. I knew I hadn't, knowing the width of the car to the nearest centimetre as any man would. She was right.

An interesting study carried out by a Dr Leon James at the University of Hawaii asked drivers to rate themselves on the one to ten scale as to how good drivers they were. Most picked nine which is fairly close to a Brooke Shields perfect ten! But in the same survey 50% admitted they speed, 70% owned up to making rude gestures at other drivers on occasion, 35% have been known to shout at other road users, and 60% admitted tail-gating. Perfect indeed! I think most readers would recognise Irish drivers in these figures. Then add in lane switching without signalling, etc. There is a lot of room for improvement, but how do we manage to believe that we are good drivers and that other road users are so bad!

James had drivers record their thoughts in the car and found that it is not so much the occupants of other cars that determine our behaviour, but the mindset the driver has which has been handed down from parent to child in typical families and not moderated by proper driver training. So, we learn that the area around our car is our space and we feel enraged if someone enters it. We learn that if a driver makes a mistake they deserve to be told (beeped at) and punished ('I'm not letting them in'). We pick the rules of the road that are okay for *us* to break as in '... this is a ridiculous place to have a STOP sign' and we ignore it. Or a speed limit. This is the car version of *à la carte* Catholicism.

We drive competitively, setting ourselves target times to get home in and are delighted to shave a few minutes off. We are also victims of a psychological trick. A videotape of lane changing showed that 70% of those who changed lanes to what they thought was a faster lane actually moved to a slower one.

What can be done to change the mindset that produces aggressive, competitive, risky, rude, careless driving? Dr James has an imaginative idea. Instead of visualising your car as a bullet making its way through traffic, think of the traffic as the circulation system of the human body where the blood keeps moving and has to get to all the vital places. Think 'how can I facilitate everyone getting to where they need to be, instead of selfishly stopping them so that I can get where I want to be a few seconds quicker'. Once you get into this co-operative driving philosophy your whole driving style changes. Everyone gets there quicker, safer and less hassled.

Still think you are a nine? Think again.

Service with a smile

I enjoy shopping. The word 'SALE' propels me into the premises and before long I am buying something that I do not need or already have. If I was rich, I would probably end up rivalling Imelda Marcos in the shoe department but sadly, I have had to become a shopper who spends more time than I want merely browsing. Like any browser, I have an ear open for eavesdropping on other people's lives. So, my ears pricked up in a Dublin shop recently when one of the people behind the till announced to her colleague, and to the entire shop, that she 'only started to come alive on the way home'.

So for the next five minutes they discussed how they lived for the night and getting 'langered'. This was interspersed with a discussion of what was the best way to do your hair before you went out. Then a lad joined with the greeting that he had seen the others on the bus but they were too 'locked' to remember him. I wondered if the state of your hair really mattered much if you are out of it, asleep with your mouth open, on the bus. The group then had a lively discussion as to who was the more 'locked' and this conversation was peppered with more 'effs' than I had heard for a while. A customer went to the till and her goods were scanned and was only addressed to tell her the total. As the woman's credit card was processed, the conversation continued unabated and when the customer went to sign she noticed that the amount was €10 less than it should be. All turned their attention to how to rectify the mistake. Only one knew how to do it and she explained it to the others, the woman signed for the correct amount, and all returned to normal.

By this time, I was full of middle-class disapproval and wondering how they could spend 90% of their money on drink. They were spending the daylight hours earning money that they would spend obliterating their brains and emotions in their leisure time. Part of me wanted to run after the woman shopper who was a tourist and apologise. But mostly I was thinking that someone, somewhere, owns this business, or has shares in it, and they are employing people who do not want to be there and who have had absolutely no training whatsoever and they are unsupervised so that they can 'eff and blind' to their hearts' content, while the customers interrupt when they want to pay for something! These people hate their jobs, see no career structure, and sadly did not seem to like the rest of their lives much either.

Later in the week, I was in America and fitted in a spot of retail therapy. I needed a new pair of running shoes so I headed down to Dick's Sporting Goods where a busy 30-something man was happily advising two sets of customers before he took me on as well. America has this image of hard sell and 'have a nice day' insincerity and there certainly is some of that around. But this employee knew every item of his stock back to front. He listened to each customer and asked about the kind of activity they were going to be doing with all the care of a heart surgeon preparing a patient to undergo the knife. For one man he had a much more suitable shoe coming in on Tuesday if he would like to wait. In chatting, we got talking about golf and he introduced me to his colleague in the golf department. Each of these people gave every appearance of enjoying their work. You got the feeling that when they went home they played football with the kids or headed out on the lake with their wife for a spot of fishing, a swim and a beer. I am sure they weren't saints either. If a good fish got away, they probably uttered an oath like the rest of us.

Someone said to me that the Irish have a bad attitude to service because of our years of oppression. Well, if so, it is high time we got over it. One of the people I dealt with was black and he had certainly as much to whinge about in the oppression department. Instead he and his colleague took pride in their work and I am now the possessor of running shoes that give me wings, a driver that only hits the ball straight (my current one has developed a fault) and a putter that cannot miss. Plus enough socks to see me down!

5

Making an Impression

The words we use – I, me, mine

We spend a lot of time talking, and very little thinking about what we say and the impression that it makes on the people who are listening to us. As we all know, we are frequently misunderstood. Half of the time we cannot understand how the other person heard something completely different from what we said.

I think it was Alice in Wonderland who believed that words could mean exactly what she wanted them to. Well in real life that doesn't work. It is much more useful to adopt the maxim that words mean whatever the listener understands them to mean rather than what the speaker wants them to mean. There are two sides to a conversation and only when there has been a big overlap do we have good communication.

Words are not just about communicating information. They are also about creating an impression, and in the end they are vital to the quality and type of relationship you form with the other person. I had this brought home to me when I viewed an exhibition of photographs from the third world a while back. As part of the exhibition, people who had visited the countries wrote a paragraph outlining their reminiscences of the visit. Two stuck in my mind.

One person used the word 'I' at least six times, with a few 'me's and 'my' thrown in. The impression created? Well, it read to me as if a self-obsessed person thought that the most interesting thing about the trip was the effect it had on them personally.

A few feet away was another short paragraph. Sprinkled though it was the word 'they'. This writer focused entirely on the people visited and the impact the project had on the lives of those living in difficult circumstances. The impression created? It is not about me. It is about them.

Which person would you prefer to sit beside at a meal? Now for all I know each are wonderful companions. But the point is that an impression is created and it does not matter what each writer meant. What matters is what the reader, or listener, picks up.

No one is going to monitor every word that comes out of their mouth, though we do usually look over letters and reports to see that they are saying what we want them to say. Conversation would be very jumpy indeed if we were running every sentence through our brains a few times before opening our mouth. But there are a few simple words we could do with more of and a few we could put on a diet.

The good words – we, us and our – are three words that bridge the gap between I and you and highlight the common ground we may share. They are inclusive words that suggest co-operation. They are words that help build good feeling and relationships. Incidentally the more you translate 'I' and 'you' to 'we' the more compelling you sound to your listener and the more persuasive you are.

The other side of the coin, the words to ration. Obviously you don't stop using them altogether but most people could do with a lot less of I, mine, you and yours. These words divide you from your listener.

Years ago when I was in Trinity College a lecturer came in and presented us with what he described an 'everyday logical puzzle' to work on for 45 minutes. We all tried it but nobody solved it. Some made more headway than others. Our lecturer looked at the efforts and remarked that some of the attempts were novel and imaginative. Some he had never seen tried before. Then he told us that it was a famous philosophical problem that had never been solved!

Had he described it that way in the beginning none of us would have even tried. Which brings me back to the words we use. Every day at work we face obstacles and problems. Or are they challenges and opportunities?

Which word is more likely to lead to a successful solution?

The gentle art of persuasion

As I have remarked there is something about the sign 'SALE' that makes me lose all normal reasoning capacity. The notion that a particular shirt is marked down an additional 30% because nobody would be seen dead in it just eludes me. Out with the plastic and off with the bargain of a lifetime. Then a few weeks later comes the event when it first sees the light of day and it is politely suggested that I change. Over the years, the thrift shops have a fair few items from me that didn't even make it to the first wash.

It seems so simple to just say 'no'. So why do we all find ourselves doing things against our better judgement and often to please somebody else who has manoeuvred us into the position? In work and life, there are plenty of people who love to sell us a pup and they usually ooze with charm while doing so. A few warm up comments about how well you are looking and most people's defences are down. From then on, you are easy pickings.

Just as the word SALE can reduce my mental powers to a rabbit staring into the headlights level, so too can some people use ploys to make us suspend all critical faculties. Recently I came across some ideas about how to spot them and save ourselves headaches, heartaches and emotional drainage. What are the signs to look for, and how will I ensure that the word SALE never again puts me in a trance?

Most people are vulnerable because they are reasonably polite and upright in their dealings and expect others to be the same. I am not saying most people don't bend a few rules and cut a few corners, but they recognise when they are doing it and it is more the exception than the rule. It is just because most of us are uncomplicated that we are easy prey to the skilled persuader. They may look the same but they are different. So watch for the following: –

You are love-bombed. A person takes an interest in you and finds all sorts of things that you have in common. Get your guard up. This may not be because they like you. It may be because you are a means to an end. The next stage is to be asked to do something with the heavy inference that you should do so 'because you like me'. Say 'no' and you have to cope with the feigned hurt. But remember, just because you like somebody doesn't mean you have to agree on everything. Beware of the amazing coincidences that you share so much in common with anybody.

Abuse of reciprocity is the next trick. Everyone can spot that person at work who gives a little and then suddenly asks for a lot in return and you are the one who feels bad. This is just what the person wants because when you feel bad you switch off some of your brain and all of the questions that you should be asking are just forgotten.

Another great phrase to get people to turn off their brains is 'everybody else is doing it'. If a teenager said it to you about alcohol you would come up with the rejoinder that if everyone is jumping off Dun Laoghaire pier would he or she do that too. But as adults, we are still often surprisingly susceptible to the feeling of being one of the crowd. Or what we are being led to believe the crowd is doing.

Another trick to be conscious of is time pressure. If someone want you to decide a particular way there is no surer way to get your critical faculties to desert you than to tell you this is a now or never opportunity. If I have to make my mind up now, then the answer is NO. Unless you want to marry in haste and repent at your leisure!

It is hard to believe that adults can so easily fall for things that they would spot across a crowded room if it was happening to someone else. But we all have done it and we keep on doing it! So, if you hear a lot of superlatives it is time to be wary. If you find yourself being impulsive and behaving out of character, it is time to be very wary indeed. If you find yourself saying that you trust somebody because they looked you straight in the eye, it is time to make your excuses and leave. Any liar worth their sale can look you straight in the eye.

Caveat emptor.

The articulate mammal – or making a chump of yourself

We have been christened the 'articulate mammal'. We are the ones who can talk as well as communicating in the more basic ways of other animals. We spend a lot of our time communicating. Sadly, we spend a good portion of that time making a right royal mess of getting our message across!

Face to face communication is when we have the opportunity to give the most information to our listener and gain the most information back about their response. But how often do you find yourself thinking 'But that is not what I meant'. Or worse than thinking it, saying it in exasperated tones. What you said and what you communicated are often two very different things.

The reason is simple. We communicate with our body language. We communicate with our tone of voice. We communicate with the words we use. But the three channels are far from equal. A mere 7% of meaning is communicated by the actual words we use. The tone of voice, and volume and speed at which we talk are far more important, delivering a hefty 38% of the meaning. This leaves 55% communicated by the body and this is the channel we read to find out about a person's feelings and attitudes. When the three channels are not sending the same message, it is the words that make the least impact.

To get your message across it is vital to have the three channels singing from the same hymn sheet. People take your tone of voice personally, so pay attention to it. Tone of voice is affected hugely by your emotional state and even if you try to hide your emotions, they tend to leak out in your voice.

But consider the further problems of our most frequent work communications – on the phone and by e-mail. Once you are on the phone the 55% is gone, and using e-mail, a further 38% is gone. So, it is very important in these two forms of communication for the other person to know clearly where you are coming from.

On the phone, the most important thing to do is simply to

talk. When the other person hears silence, they do not know what is going on. You may be smiling at their amusing conversation but if you say nothing they don't know that. Each of the yeses, OKs and uh-huhs let the other person know that you are listening and from your tone of voice they get information about how you are responding emotionally. Going back over something they have said lets them know you were fully hearing them. Taking brief notes is a help. But only of the conversation. If you are trying to do two things at once and sorting out your diary at the same time the other person will sense your disinterest. So, practise your meaningful grunts!

Think about your posture. You talk differently if you are relaxed with your feet up to when you are hunched over a desk, or walking around the room.

But if you have to work harder on the phone to avoid confusion you have to think even more carefully with the e-mail where the 38% communicated by the voice is gone. Think back to first principles. It is vital that the person knows where you are coming from if they are to understand your words correctly. The context matters and you have to make it clear. So, begin your e-mails with a sentence explaining your intentions so that they know the appropriate attitude to take to the words. End with a clear statement of how you intend the e-mail to be used. Do you expect a reply? Is there something they should do? Or perhaps it is intended for information only.

Words are powerful. But the context is what gives them clear meaning. So, take a minute to think about your emotions, attitudes and intentions before setting to work with your words. You will be a more articulate animal.

Listen up!

'You haven't heard a single word I've said. Have you?' However much you protest and try to cover yourself, both you and your loved one, or maybe parent, know the truth. Your mind was elsewhere.

We can all instantly transport ourselves back to the classroom just by hearing the sentence – 'Masterson, stand up and tell the class what I have just said'. Any adult can feel the fear and remember days when the only thing on their mind that particular history class was that *Sergeant Pepper* was just out and you had to get it that afternoon. Or would you pluck up the courage to speak to Avril if you engineered it to pass her in the corridor at lunch?

It happens at work too. When was the last time you had a row at work because you weren't paying any attention to the person who was earnestly telling you something you needed to know. Remember the last time you were on the receiving end of 'No, actually that wasn't what I said at all. What I said was …' and your nose is rubbed in it for the next few minutes and you try not to look too sheepish.

Today's world is a cacophony of messages bombarded at us from the television, newspapers, the radio, phones, car horns and people, so in general it is not surprising that we hear only about half of what is said to us. We listen to only half of that, and we remember about half of what we listen to. Do the sums and it is apparent that only about one-eighth of what is addressed to us actually gets in.

Countless books have been written about the importance of how we present ourselves and communicate to get our message across making the best use of our verbal and non-verbal language. But less emphasis has been paid to the skill of listening, and it is a skill. Poor listening is an enormous time waster and the cause of much aggravation to the people we deal with both at home and at work.

When people talk of the great listeners, they stress the 'lock on' contact that you feel from the person. Bill Clinton is legendary for his ability to make you feel that you have his total attention, that you are the most important person in his universe, and that he is hearing and understanding exactly what you are saying in all its nuances. Anyone whom Gay Byrne ever interviewed knows what total interest in you feels like.

Communicating that you genuinely understand is the key to good listening because that is the ingredient that makes the speaker feel empathy and that is a special feeling. The speaker feels that you are actually able to put yourself in their shoes, to genuinely see things from their perspective.

People often scoff at the stereotyped therapist who makes good eye contact, nods and says 'uh-huh' every now and again. But these are essential listening skills. Think of how often you do the opposite and, in particular, how often you are not listening to what the person is saying to you because your whole attention is on what *you* will say next irrespective of what is being said to you and which you haven't heard anyway!

A good way to keep engaged on the other person is to summarise back to them what you have just heard them say. The trick is to identify the core of their message and give it back to them in your own words. You might restate a crucial word in what they said to make sure you understood. Do it skilfully and they will feel heard. On occasion, it will lead to further discussion to refine a point.

You will be surprised to realise when you really listen how much you were missing up to now. Most times, you were hearing the chaff and missing the wheat.

Tone deaf

There are some people who we approach with caution because we know that every word we utter will be parsed and analysed and the chances of them reacting in a way that we had not anticipated, or do not want, are high. It may be a difficult person at work that you have to reprimand. It may even be that difficult person at work who you want to praise. It happens in our personal relationships too when we say something and it is taken up wrongly and before you know it you are in a bad-tempered exchange, mentally scratching your head wondering where all this came from and what did you do to deserve it. All you said was 'would you like to go out to dinner on Wednesday?' and suddenly the Third World War has begun because you were callous enough to forget that Wednesday was a particularly important night for him/her for a reason that had totally slipped your mind. In fact, Wednesday didn't matter a damn to you. It could just have easily have been any other day. Nor did dinner matter. Going to a film, or for a walk or whatever would have been fine. All you were trying to say was that it would be nice to go out together during the week. But that is not what you got across.

Often the words are not very important. It is the tone and intent of your communication that matters. Tone is important because you want to sound like you mean what you are saying. Making your intent clear is important because it lessens the chances of the other person picking it up wrongly and the two of you going into a downward spiral before you can stop it.

We all know that tone of voice is important when we are on the receiving end, but we are usually less conscious of our own tone of voice. The circumstances we are in have a big impact on how we sound. If you make a social arrangement in the middle of a busy work day, you will probably sound very matter of fact and cold. You will be rushed and will just tick off the box in exactly the same manner as dozens of other tasks you perform that day. Often people will just recognise that you are in 'work mode' and may take no offence and even joke about it later. Often, but not always.

People tend to take tone of voice personally, even if the tone you adopt has absolutely nothing whatsoever to do with them. It could be as a result of a row you just had, or at the other end of the spectrum because of a joke you just heard. But for the listener it is all they hear and they assume it is to do with them.

When words and tone are saying different things, the resulting mixed message is likely to cause conflict. It may be that you are trying to hide your real feelings but feelings can leak out and it is often heard in your tone of voice. Or it may be that you are just hassled, or depressed, or giddy, but it still leaks out. As a rule, people will respond to the tone and ignore the words, and if you have any doubt about that imagine yourself on the receiving end again and the penny will drop.

The other vital clue to give to people is your intent. It gives them a context in which to hear what you are saying. Many meanings can be taken from every conversation, and by prefacing what you say you can get them into the same ballpark as you are in. Most people pay little or no attention to making sure that their intent is clear. We all know when we are talking to someone on the same wavelength and explaining our intent would seem silly. But likewise we all know times when we are having a tough time getting the other person to hear what we are saying and it is probable that our intent is not clear. So, in a difficult communication it is useful to ask yourself what is your real purpose in the conversation and to think of a way to make that clear to the other person. They may not like what you have to say, but at least they know where you are coming from, and the chances of a decent two-way conversation are greatly increased.

6

Confidence – The New God

Party animals

The Christmas party time of year fills many people with dread. For most of us, the thought of going into a room where cool, funny, happy people are enjoying themselves and setting about mingling is a little daunting. For some it is pure hell. We have all had the experience of being on the edge of a group and no one noticing you exist. Or being included and making a *faux pas* in your first few words. Or telling a joke that fell flat, you made a mess of, or was completely misjudged for the company. We have spent entire nights talking to the person we went with as if there was no tomorrow and wishing we had had that chat somewhere more conducive, like a restaurant. Or the zoo. We have all had bizarre conversations that make us feel very foolish indeed. I remember once realising to my horror that for the past five minutes the remainder of the group were talking about Wales while I was taking about 'whales'. There was no recovery. At best, they thought I was a bit odd. More likely, they decided on very stupid.

We have been at parties where boring people clung to us like limpets. We have been at parties where we bored people to death and did not know how to move on and inflict ourselves on a new victim. What it all comes down to are three skills which hardly anyone possesses naturally but which most of us can improve. Firstly there is how to join a group of people who are chatting, then how to maintain a conversation that is at least mildly interesting, and finally how to take our leave and move on to chat with others. These three skills make up the noble art of 'mingling'.

It is the first of these three that gives people most concern, the 'how to get started'. It is probably worth mentioning that whoever gives a party has some responsibility to ensure that people there meet people and are introduced. It is up to the individual to make the most of the opportunity but it is just plain rude to take someone's coat, put a drink in their hand, and then let them fend for themselves.

Remember, you were invited because somebody liked you and

wanted you in their house. The other thing to remember is that there are other people there who are feeling just as awkward as you are. Even the most socially accomplished people will admit to having to make an effort to overcome what they see as their natural shyness. So, it begins with effort. If you fake it, you will start to feel it. Looking happy is a good way to begin to feel happy. Looking pleased to be there may turn into being pleased to be there. Remember the purpose of going to a party is to have fun.

People often make derogatory remarks about the small talk made at parties. But if you don't go through some of it you don't have the opportunity to meet someone you might genuinely like and want to meet again. Small talk is trivial meaningless conversations – so what! It beats standing with your back to the wall looking glum!

When you go into a room, you will spot the party 'star' group laughing loudly, full of confidence and sure they are the centre of attention. Don't go for the high rollers. Far safer to pick out the saddest bunch in the room and practise your skills. They will probably be delighted to talk to you. It also helps if you can identify someone similar to you in some way. It makes conversation easier to have something in common. Mothers can find mothers. Golfers can find golfers. Smokers can certainly find smokers. Beware of asking people what they do in life too early. It smacks of trying to position them socially and often comes out sounding all wrong.

Practise your party skills in a secure environment. In an office party where you know a lot of people make the effort to talk to someone new. At a family gathering, seek out a neighbour you don't know. Remember that when you make the effort someone who is even shyer than you will see you as a godsend.

If nothing else comes to mind you might risk honesty – 'excuse me but I don't know a single person here' – and introduce yourself.

Shrinking Violets

I was driving up and down country lanes with a friend during the summer and we were totally lost. Eventually we came to a small filling station and I asked her to go and get directions while I tried to make head or tail of the map. 'Oh, I'd rather not,' she said, 'I'm not very good at that sort of thing'. I got out of the car in a less than pleasant disposition and before long we were on our way. But I did not have the common sense to let the matter rest there. How could she not be able to ask directions? It just didn't add up to me. Then this perfectly normal woman explained to me that it was a shyness problem and that she just felt very uncomfortable about talking to people she didn't know for the first time.

I'm shy too, I thought, but I just get on with it. I was walking through Trinity College recently and was transported back to how I was as a 19 year old. Today I stroll across the cobblestones enjoying the sunshine and admiring the buildings. Then I wouldn't have walked across the middle of front square to escape a fire. My heart would have pounded. I would have been conscious of every muscle in my body. I would have been quite convinced that people behind every window had stopped what they were doing to look at the clumsy being walking out in the open and would probably have discussed me with anyone willing to listen. I would have avoided all that by scurrying around the edges of the square with my head down where I could only be seen by people at one side. OK, I exaggerate a bit, but like many adolescents, I was dreadfully self-conscious and like most people, I grew out of it and can't remember when or how.

Shy people seem to imagine that a spotlight is focused on them and that they are the centre of unwelcome attention. What we fail to realise, though it only takes a moment to understand, is that people have plenty of other things on their mind which are far more important to them. So, primarily, people are far less attentive to us than we, and in particular shy people, think.

The other thing that shy people do is to magnify the importance of the many little social mistakes we make every day. We all forget names, pronounce words wrongly, and walk into rooms with ice cream on our jackets now and again. The shy person assumes that the people who see and hear them think that they are a total fool. But the chances are that other people judge us far less harshly than we fear, and in most cases have forgotten about it in no time and moved on to something else. Shy people focus on themselves and not on the people around them. They receive positive information about themselves but often do not process it. Usually people take credit for their successes and blame their failures on outside forces, but shy people do just the opposite.

In some cases, the effects of shyness can have a damaging effect on the person's life. The job interview can be a nightmare for someone whose heart pounds, mouth dries and sentences just won't come out. Failure multiplies the problem as the person collects evidence that they must be right about being stupid. Psychologists sometimes lump these behaviours with difficulty in many social situations and term it 'social anxiety disorder', thankfully a condition that can soon be reversed with some counselling and training.

Researchers see shyness as a continuum and the surprising thing is that almost everybody reports feeling shy at least some of the time, and approximately half of the adults in one study described themselves as shy 'most of the time'. Only a small percentage of the population, less than 5%, are chronically shy all of the time to a degree that it is having a major negative effect on their lives. But as many as one in five are what are termed 'shy extroverts', people who seem to be outgoing and sociable but report feeling shy underneath. Just like my friend in the car.

It is comforting to know that we are shyer animals than most of us think. There is nothing wrong with standing back a little rather than rushing confidently into every situation. But if it is reaching a stage that it is seriously cramping your style, remember that it is mostly in your head, and a little help will move you along the continuum to a more enjoyably social place.

I can do that

'I can solve most problems if I put in the necessary effort.' Does that sound like you? Or this? 'I can deal efficiently with unexpected events.' Are you one of those people who can handle whatever life throws in your direction? Can you rise above negative remarks another person may make about you? If you are answering 'yes' to these questions then you are one of those lucky people who are high in self-belief, a hugely important quality for achieving success in any walk of life. People who score low on these questions are much more likely to complain about their health, to suffer from stress related problems, including depression, and to feel burned out. When people high on self-efficacy encounter health problems and undergo surgery they recover more quickly.

What separates the winning sportsman from the also ran? Often their physical and technical abilities do not differ. But at the psychological level, the winner has a self-belief that makes the difference. It is sometimes referred to as a positive mental attitude, an 'I can do that' approach to life. Apparently, we 'talk' to ourselves over 45,000 times a day. While lots of that talk is trivial like wondering what is on the television, much of it is comment about ourselves so it is important to keep the positive proportion high.

What we believe about ourselves influences how we behave. Our beliefs cause us to notice some things and completely miss others. If we believe that people naturally like us unless we do something to make them dislike us, we will approach personal relations very differently from believing that people will not like us unless we do something special to deserve their affection. Children form beliefs of this type from what they are told by adults and childhood is an important time to build up a natural self-confidence. Beliefs, positive and negative, set off a cycle. A person who radiates confidence on entering a room is seen as capable, a good motivator, and the response that person gets further builds up their confidence.

Sometimes you have to fake it. The public speaker before going out in front of a crowd takes a deep breath and walks on the stage smiling, shoulders back and looking like they are delighted to be there and feeling just as comfortable as could be. As anyone who performs in public or addresses groups of people will tell you in those first few minutes they are usually quaking inside and putting on an act. Then as they see the audience respond, they feel more at home until the act is no longer needed. They are in their stride, in the moment and enjoying the buzz. Their public and private selves may be different to begin with but before long, they are the same.

There are limits to self-belief. There is no sense in playing mind games and believing you can do a mile in 3 minutes 45 seconds and be a supermodel next week. That is not belief. It is delusion. But there are substantial changes we can make in our beliefs about ourselves and that process will in turn increase our chances of achieving goals. Our beliefs can be springboards or straitjackets – they can guide us happily to a goal, or ensure that we haven't a snowball's chance in hell of getting there.

So how do you go about changing a self-limiting belief about yourself to a more positive outlook? First, identify an area of your life that you feel could do with some improvement. Now write down what you would like to be. Do it in a short simple sentence that anyone could understand, make it positive, and say it to yourself in the present as if it is already part of you.

For the shy person it could be 'I enjoy meeting people'. For the couch potato 'I enjoy my lunchtime walk'. Keep it simple and achievable. Make yourself comfortable, close your eyes and speak the words to yourself. Unbelievably it works.

If you don't believe what you are saying you will find reasons to fail. So, try on some positive beliefs about yourself and see if they fit. It is your beliefs that produce life's experiences a lot more than the other way around.

Teachers for life

Anyone who has watched Kildare football for the past few years knows what a difference a good coach makes. The talents of Mick O'Dwyer were applied to the local talent and the team made enormous strides. Now we watch what he is doing for Laois.

An Italian friend of mine had a long-time weight problem. He is an intelligent man who had succeeded in just about everything he ever did. Except lose weight. He had tried everything. Then two years ago I met a very much slimmed down version of the same man and a happier man! So how had he done it? He had a personal trainer who just made him do the exercise. And such was the commitment both had to the project that in the middle of a five-day conference the trainer arrived off the plane to keep my friend on the right road. It seemed extravagant to me at the time, but looking at the big picture it was well worth it.

In recent years, more and more people are turning to life coaches to help them get things done that they just don't seem to be able to get done themselves. People often get the feeling that life is passing them by and that one year is becoming little more than a repeat of the last. All around we hear people saying that life isn't a rehearsal, and this forces people to question whether they are making the best use of the three-score-and-ten-year visit to this world.

Coaching grew out of counselling when it became apparent to many therapists that ordinary everyday people were consuming self-help books in vast quantities. These were not people who needed problems in their past sorted out. They were people who were going through the normal vicissitudes of an ever more complex social and work world and needed some guidance and signposts. Some were a bit stressed out. Some were having difficulty setting goals and achieving them. All were normal people and so out of therapy coaching was born and the success of the new practice was transmitted largely by word of mouth.

Coaching is a relationship between two people, the coach and the client. They may meet face to face or, more often, talk on the telephone once a week. The focus of every session is on seeing where you are now and establishing where it is you want to be. By summer, I would wager that most people's New Year resolutions are well and truly abandoned. The coach assists the person to set realistic attainable goals. People are usually much better at identifying what they do not want to be than what they do want to be so a little guidance in this area can prove very fruitful. The life coach then motivates them so that they do more changing for themselves than they would if left to their own devices. The coach will sharpen the client's focus enabling them to get results quicker. In summary, the coach is a resource who has the experience to provide the tools, structure and support to help the client accomplish more. Coaching doesn't change people but it helps them to see more choices and options so that they can change themselves. It is a bit like having your life 'serviced'. You can gain a fuller sense of where your life is going and what it is you value.

The areas people want to change are manifold. It may be related to work, relationships, physical well-being, a new hobby or a project that just has not been done. Instead of focusing on why you are where you are, the coach will be forward looking and bringing resources from all aspects of your life to get you to a new goal. If that feels a bit self-indulgent ask yourself how much you would pay to get some of the life changes you desire. You will probably conclude that a little expert help is worthwhile. Why is it that no one would build a house without consulting the appropriate professionals but are happy to let life drift from day to day, until the weeks become months and finally years?

Coaching is a relationship in which you will be challenged. To get anywhere you will need to be committed but on your way, the support and guidance will be useful.

Best foot forward

Padraic Harrington is 80 yards from the hole. He needs to get down in two. You've watched him walk up the fairway and you are ready to put your last €100 on him. There is a 50-yard lake in front of him and he hardly sees it. He has a wedge in his hand, takes a good look, pops the ball up in the air and it finishes six feet from the hole. Will the putt roll into the middle of the hole? You can be sure of it.

It is all about confidence and he oozes it. It is in the walk, in the talk, in the look. Of course, it has something to do with the hours of practice, the dedication and his physical condition. But they are all small beer compared to the magic of confidence. He really believes he can land the ball on a sixpence.

When you are feeling good about yourself, the bounces go your way. When feeling down it seems as if nothing can go right.

With the magic ingredient, people can move mountains. The self-confident person has faith in their abilities and ideas. They tend to be happy, healthy, productive and successful. So how can we get a bit more of it? For those of us who get a dose of the January blues how can we get it back quickly? There is probably more to it than just using the right toothpaste!

Like most thing it begins in childhood. Praise is the oxygen that makes it flourish, and criticism is about as useful as Roundup. Remember, 'catch the child being good'. Honest praise is the quickest way to build self-confidence and even if there is plenty you do not like there is always something to be positive about.

Once the parental foundations are in place, a child's social world expands and the comments of friends and teachers become important influences. In the teenage years, we all know how vital the peer group becomes. The self-confident child is far better equipped to make up its own mind in the context of peer pressure.

Just acting more confident has an effect. Your mother wasn't far wrong with that advice to stand up straight. Watch the confident person enter a room. They will be relaxed, head held up and smiling. They radiate energy and warmth. They transmit a 'feel good' atmosphere to all around. People find these personal qualities a lot more attractive than the more superficial things like fashionably good looks and a body to match. The confident person is irresistible.

We all feel down at times, but we have the mental abilities to improve our lot. Just a few minutes focusing on times when things were good will give us a lift. Imagining the impression you want to make and rehearsing it in your head can make it that much easier to do. It is a bit like laughter. It always makes you feel better and look better.

The impressions we make on other people are important to us and the impressions we make stick in the other person's mind. It is your choice whether you want to come across as mousy. Or make an entrance. It is like happiness. Somebody said to me recently that nobody can make you happy. Most people are about as happy as they make up their minds to be.

So throw the shoulders back, take a deep breath and put your best foot forward and you may just find you are making the kind of impression you dreamed about. It won't always work, but anything is better than making so little impact that people barely recall your name.

One more point. When Padraic Harrington dumps one in the water, as he occasionally does, he just dusts himself off and gets on with it. Learn from the past, but don't be trapped by it. You can only influence now and the future.

7

Office Dynamics and Dynamic Offices

Your boss is half your age

It is part of being middle-aged. Increasingly I hear of people who are suddenly in the situation of having a bright young thing half their age as their new boss. Sometimes it works fine. Sometimes it is a disaster. I think I am probably the least ageist of people. I can effortlessly think of people 20 years older than me who have accomplished more by Monday evening than most people manage in a week. I couldn't care less if I was working for a teenager if they knew what they were doing. That is often at the heart of whether or not the arrangement works.

Competent people are are not plagued by insecurity. People who are competent gain respect easily from others. Does anyone on the Irish team mind being captained by Brian O'Driscoll? I think not. Probably the person most concerned by Brian O'Driscoll being captain was himself. It was an honour proffered because of his ability. But he would have seen it as a responsibility and a challenge that he was determined to discharge successfully. We know what happened. For a bonus, he made Bertie cry! It looked to me as if Tom McGurk had a good fill of emotion when the final whistle blew and the World Champions had been given a lesson at Twickenham.

Yes. Age, sex, race, whatever, all diminish in importance when the person knows what they are at. You cannot imagine hearing Brian O'Driscoll saying 'you'll do it because I say so. I am the captain'. He wouldn't last long.

If you ever hear someone using their job title to demand that something be done then you are probably looking at someone who is unsure about his or her competence and is falling back on whatever power they have. For the time being. Far better, the person who listens to all points of view and then, almost reluctantly, accepts the mantle of responsibility and makes the decision that everyone will have to live with.

We do hear horror stories of young people promoted who almost immediately overstep the mark by throwing their weight around and in general making people's lives a misery with 'do this' and 'do that' and just not being satisfied with anybody or anything. Rest assured you are dealing with somebody who deep down worries that they are not up to the job.

How do you help them through it and in the process get them off your back? If the root is their confidence then help them feel confident. Don't behave like a puppet, but make sure they know your number one aim is that everyone higher up in the company is going to see that the new appointment works. You are on the same team.

Sometimes the same team can become a little too familiar. Have you ever been in the situation where your much younger boss wants to chat over coffee about their relationship problems, or successes, or how they spend the weekend, or how their parents are driving them mad? If so, you know the pitfalls. If not, make your excuses and leave. This familiarity can turn and bite you in an instant. Some day it will dawn on the bright young thing that they have disclosed too much and the only way to deal with this is to cut you off. You have done nothing wrong.

You work together. You don't have to be best friends.

As workplaces become more casual and the old hierarchies break down, it is becoming all the more common to have a mixture of sexes, age groups, races, religions and senses of style. Sexist men have had to come to terms with reporting to women and some still wish they were born 50 years earlier. But gradually the personal qualities that we are born with are overtaken by ambition and ability. Sometimes the workplace is taking on the apparent friendliness of a cafeteria!

Don't be fooled. If there is a big difference in status, ability or age between you and your new 'friend', tread carefully. It may turn out fine, but work is first of all about work and if you remember that you might avoid a few of those minefields that are put there to try us. I think it was Henry Kissinger who remarked that the office politics in some institutions are particularly vicious because the stakes are so low.

Meetings ... meetings ... meetings
include me out

I am always glued to the radio when I hear someone venting their spleen on the subject of committees. I am not a fan and have entirely the wrong personality to spend time with many people inching towards a decision. Mind you, I do not have to turn down many invitations to join such bodies because any sensible person wouldn't want me on their committee. My heart goes out to politicians who spend their lives at this sort of thing. Whatever they are paid, it isn't enough. Though we could do with a few less of them.

However in the course of my work I do have to attend a reasonable number of meetings with anything from two to a dozen people present. The smaller they are the more I like them. The more focused they are the better. But I have had the experience of working effectively with a large group of people with a common purpose and a number of simple things seemed to contribute to the effectiveness of the group.

Firstly, it matters a lot that the appropriate time is set aside for whatever tasks are to be accomplished. If there is not enough work to fill the time people are less interested in the next get together and motivation and productivity wanes and people who love the sound of their own voice will fill the time.

Likewise, if there is not sufficient time allocated, things that may be of particular importance to some of the people present are not addressed. They have wasted their time and in today's world time is the one thing we have too little of.

A good chairperson makes a big difference in constructing an agenda that is achievable in the time set aside and ensuring that the correct people are present to move things forward. Any undertakings people make to do things should be realistic. There is no point in someone offering the sun moon and stars if they are not going to deliver. A good leader sets the atmosphere of the group and the members soon get to know what is expected of them. A climate is created where everyone feels free to say what they have to say and feel secure about it. The good chairperson ensures that decisions are made and understood. Procrastination is the thief of time and if there are 10 people at the table that is a lot of time stolen.

There are some people who seem to love meetings and I often think they use them as an excuse for not doing any other work. They are eternally 'at meetings'. In my experience, these self-same people love to contribute their thoughts even when they are entirely irrelevant. The good chairperson can shorten their contributions without squashing them. But how often have you walked out of a room after a fruitless hour wondering 'what was that all about? I have better things to do'. We all have and we don't enjoy it.

In my experience, and this is something of a vast generalisation, women are more efficient at running and contributing to meetings than men. It seems that less of their ego is caught up in work and this must be related to the fact that the sharing of household tasks still is not within an ass' roar of 50–50 so women are less inclined to waste time at work. They want to accomplish what needs to be accomplished, but their workplace has none of the features of a club as it seems to do for some men.

For maximum satisfaction you need a realistic agenda, one that the people present all have a stake in so they feel they need to be there, enough time to thrash out the issues, allocate the tasks, and get things done.

It always helps to start on a positive note. For the boss to be secure enough to ask what they can do to assist always makes a difference. Nobody might take them up, but the offer matters and it radiates a confidence that is infectious.

Many hands make light work – maybe, maybe not

Just as people have personalities so do groups of people. For a group of people to do what they are supposed to do requires that the individual personalities that make up the group dynamic blend well rather than pull against each other. Whether at work, in a sports club, on a committee or running a church fundraiser we can all think of experiences when a group of people have worked together enjoyably and well, and we can definitely all think of times when if they were trying to organise a mountain walk people would have ended up on three different mountains.

Just as no two families are alike, no two groups are alike. Each time a group is formed, the personalities blend in a unique way. Someone joining or leaving can have a huge impact on the atmosphere and on the effectiveness.

We don't choose our family and often one's role in the family is very clear because of age, sex, personality and ability. That role can stay very stable over years. But we can choose, to a greater degree, the groups we are part of. If they are to do with work, we have a group of adults who have a great deal of latitude as to how they will behave. How you behave with the group who organise a holiday trip may be very different from how you behave in a project group at work.

As adults, we are aware that our personality changes from one situation to another. The quiet person in the corner may be the life and soul of the party elsewhere. If we just leave things to chance when we are part of a group of people, we have little influence over the outcome. Instead, we can ask ourselves which of our personalities are the most agreeable for us, and which are the most troublesome? If you are honest, I think everyone can think of a relationship that they approached in one way and, if they could only have stepped back for a moment to have a look at themselves, would have been able to choose a far more effective way. Sometimes an apology will repair the damage. Sometimes the train is on the tracks and you cannot turn back. But you do have a choice.

With a group, as with most things in life, the old maxim *tús maith, leath na hoibre* – a good start is half the work – holds well. First and foremost there needs to be a clear and agreed understanding about what the task in hand is. There will always be jockeying for position and trying to carve out a role for oneself in the early stages of a group's work, but there will be far less friction if everyone is pointed in the same direction.

A group will work effectively when there is general agreement about the aims and when people have a clear understanding of how they can contribute and assist each other. Each person also needs to feel confident that they can challenge the way things are going if necessary.

As time passes a number of destructive personality traits can emerge that it is well worth keeping an eye out for. The dictator who will not listen, the person who acts the victim or martyr, and the person whose contributions usually judge others can cause havoc. Many people have difficulty dealing with leadership and authority and a skilled manager needs to identify people who cause trouble in this area. They can spread discontent faster than the winter hospital bug. If you yourself have a clear view about how you deal with authority, you will save yourself many difficulties in your interpersonal relations. Give it a moment's thought.

A few simple things destroy the pleasure and effectiveness of any group. One is if people start giving lectures. Rest assured that everyone else is turned off and a lot of energy is going to waste. Another is if people are given no space or time to thrash out issues that are arising along the way. If concerns are not dealt with, they will fester. Thirdly, any perception of cliques and hidden agendas will rapidly destroy the commitment and common purpose that are essential to cohesion.

Instead, try listening when people are talking. Curb your desire to give other people unasked-for advice. Be open about where you are coming from. Keep a clear eye on where you are going and you might just get there and enjoy the trip.

Select the best for a winning team

Have you ever wondered how some people got the job they are doing? Probably every day of your life. We all know of situations where even the dogs in the street could work out that the person in question is entirely unsuited for the job they are doing.

So how did they get there? In all probability, they were interviewed, and if there is a more unreliable way of picking people for a job it has yet to be put into widespread use. This is in part because people who are not trained in interviewing skills carry out most interviews. It is also because, in many cases, they are not sure precisely what they are looking for, and finally, even if they know what they want they may not be able to recognise it if it is staring them in the face.

This is further exacerbated because lots of people think they are good interviewers, and whether they are or not does not usually become apparent because nobody checks on how well their selections are working out. There would usually be a panel to share the blame in any case.

But interviewing has one great asset. It is cheap. Well maybe not cheap, but it appears to be when compared with more exhaustive alternatives. Again, I say appears to be because no one counts the costs of the 'mistakes' that are employed.

It was with these considerations in mind that I joined my production team-mates at Coco Television and embarked with vigour on the task of selecting 16 *Treasure Island* contestants from the thousands upon thousands of hopeful applicants. Did it matter if we got it right? It mattered big time. Nobody was going to thank us if we put a bunch of 'woodeners' on national television.

So to get it right is time-consuming and expensive, and the first step in filling any job vacancy is knowing what is needed. We were looking for people to represent today's Ireland. They needed strong personalities as even the greatest live wire becomes quiet after three days without food. They needed to be intelligent enough to solve clues, fit enough for the physical tasks, able to get on with people, and able to stand up for themselves. A sense of humour or the ability to entertain is a bonus, as well as the possession of many other skills and qualities that make for good television. Suffice it to say we had a checklist of what we were looking for.

For the office equivalent how many interviewers has a checklist of the skills, experience, personal attributes, etc., that they would ideally like in a potential employee? I wonder.

For *Treasure Island* stage one was a detailed application form, all of which were read. Next, several hundred were selected for a structured telephone interview. Many fell by the wayside as they looked great on paper but couldn't deliver on the phone. The resulting smaller group were video taped and it is always fascinating that the person who is strong on paper and who bounces out of the telephone many not bounce off the screen. Finally, we were down to 22 who are all given a comprehensive psychological assessment to screen out people who might have difficulty enduring the harsh environment of *Treasure Island* and the psychological demands of reality television. These 22 were then put through two days of physical, mental and roughing it tests before the final 8 men and 8 women emerged.

For an employer it is important to build up as full a picture as possible of the candidates' strengths and weaknesses as if the wrong decision is made the mistake will be very difficult and costly to rectify. Can they do the job and what is your evidence? How will they get on with workmates and how do you know? Is their level of motivation and ambition suited to the job and what are you basing that on?

Did we get it right? I think all of our team are fully in agreement. These castaways were loved, admired, trusted and distrusted, liked and disliked, identified with or not even viewed as members of the same species. We wondered would there be any romantic interest. Yes, there was a marriage two years later. None of us can claim to have predicted that!

The office ogres – control freaks and attention seekers

You drive into work without a care. Gerry Ryan is being outrageously funny and you have tears running down your cheeks. Stopped at the lights you can see two other people who just have to be listening to the same programme. You pull in to your car park and look around for a vacant spot. Then you see it. Your heart sinks. The 'ogre' is back.

Just as there are people who can make you feel good by their very presence there are people who can bring you down. They don't even have to be present. Just the thought that they are in the building, even in the same postal district, is enough to put you in a bad mood. You realise that for the last three weeks when he/she had been on holidays, or even the last two days when he/she had been on a trip, work had been a pleasant place to be.

No more. So how do we deal with the people who have such a negative effect on us? What can we do to stop them getting to us? There probably isn't a lot we can do to change them but there is a little. So by and large, we have to refuse to allow them get to us.

Let's keep it simple. There are two main types of people who are possessed with that ability to drive all around them mad. First, there are the control freaks and the many varieties of them from demanding to dominating to bullying. Secondly, there are the attention seekers who will upset any apple cart just to bring the spotlight back to them.

So how do you deal with the foaming at the mouth, demanding supervisor whose every word is designed to chip away more of your confidence? As far as they are concerned, they have right on their side. Everything they are saying is both true and obvious and only a fool like you wouldn't realise this. It is all for the good of the company and their job would be so much easier if they didn't have to cope with the likes of you. Once they are on a rant, they go on and on and reason doesn't enter into it. If you try to interrupt, they just speak faster and louder and squash you further.

There is one thing you need to keep in mind when dealing with these people. It is 'self-respect'. You are entitled to it and don't let anyone take it away. Remember that the people who treat you like this are usually quite unhappy in themselves and frequently have a great deal of anger about life eating them up. So feel a little sorry for them first and that takes away some of the fear. They are usually emotionally immature and often a bit pathetic.

But you can't tell them that so what do you do apart from imagining them in their underwear to lighten your load? First, decide you will not be walked on. Then you need to be heard to get your point across. The best way to stop them is to use their name. It is far better than 'but' or 'hold on a minute'. They are self-centred and they like their name.

Once you have their attention return to their central point and that point only. They will have strayed far from it. If they rant, again repeat the procedure. Then finally leave them a little bit of room to move at the end. They are entitled to their self-respect too. God knows they need it. Despite all the forcefulness, they are frequently quite fragile people. Sometimes it helps to end by asking them a question that you know they will have a clear answer to.

Next to the attention seekers are the ones who always chip in with the undermining comment to the know-it-alls who love the sound of their own voice. Try giving them the attention they so much crave. Not when they demand it but when you decide to give it. Get there before them and you may discover they are better friends than foes. Even if you can't stand the sight of them!

Then there is the day that you see a flier on the wall announcing drinks for them on Friday. They are heading off to pastures new.

Oh happiness. Oh unbounded joy. I won't turn up but I'll drink to their success. Elsewhere!

A bad attitude

Is there anything harder to deal with on a day-to-day basis at work than someone who displays a 'bad attitude'? Is there anything harder to put your finger on despite the fact that everyone from the cleaning staff, to the customers, to the boss can sense it during their waking hours, and if they are unlucky have nightmares about it during their sleeping hours?

Attitude problems come in a variety of shades, all negative. They sometimes come under the guise of good motivation in that the person in question 'only wants the best' for the company – it is just that everyone else is on a disaster course and needs that pointed out to them at every available opportunity. There may be 99 things going the right direction but rest assured this person will home in on the one questionable thing and pick over its entrails forever rather than get on with the things about which they have no quarrel. I did read of one company who turned this on its head by presenting every draft plan to their most negative employee and asking them to look for all the holes in it before it went any further. At least then they were more likely to put their weight behind the finished product.

When people turn sour, there is usually something negative in their history that made them change. Large organisations are particularly prone to these types of people and anyone who works in one can think of people who seemed to undergo a character transformation over the years. It may be that they were passed over for a job they wanted. It may be coming to terms with friends or family doing better that they are. It may be an unhappy home life. It may be that they are uneasy about change. Whatever it is it shows in the same way. You will constantly hear that the company is run by fools who have no idea what they are doing and are probably only feathering their own nests. Every innovation is a stupid idea and was done far better, or 'properly', years ago.

There is no point in agreeing with them because it only encourages them, or disagreeing because they can go on forever. They will be far more expert at being negative than you ever could be at being positive. But remember, they are not intending to make you miserable, even if they do.

The more difficult attitude problem is the person who is capable of being difficult and contrary as well as negative. These people seem to get a perverse pleasure out of being awkward. They seem to be resentful of the world and everything in it. What can you do?

First of all, look to yourself. Have you ever treated them in a way that gave rise to this resentment which then festered? Next, you should listen to what other people have to say and try and get facts rather than just eyes turned towards heaven. Once you have satisfied yourself that what people are suffering is far beyond the normal person's ability to irritate on an occasional basis you know you have an attitude problem to deal with.

Confronting the person is difficult because you are making a personal comment which they will probably deny. If you cite what others have said, without naming names, make it clear that you asked them. They did not come running to you.

Tell them your experience of them. Tell them that you do not want to listen to grumbling about work and people. Do your best to be open to a reason. If there is a real problem, you may be able to help, or at least be sympathetic.

But the bottom line is that if they want to be miserable and wear it on their sleeve all the time you do not have to put up with it. It is entirely reasonable to expect certain standards of behaviour from workmates or employees. They can do what they like at home, but no one is paid enough to have to work, and put up with bad vibes all day.

Make a decision - any decision - please

She was a very talented young television researcher and she was walking towards me with flames in her eyes and smoke coming out of her ears. 'I need a cup of coffee', was all she said and I knew better than to decline. So we sat down and she poured it out in one sentence – 'Heaven deliver me from men who can't make a decision'.

She had five items on the go and knew for sure that they would not all get on air. But she couldn't get any guidance concerning which ones to concentrate on and which to drop. Keeping that many balls in the air, and stringing along the people involved with each story, had gone beyond a joke.

'At this stage I'd be happy to be told they were all rubbish', was her last sentence before she managed to get back her normal smile and approach to life.

Decisions keep an organisation moving. When they are not being made at the appropriate time a logjam develops and frustration spreads like wildfire. The decisions don't even have to be the right one. Though it is obviously better if they are. They just have to be made so that people can get on with whatever they are getting on with.

Decisive people know that there are no perfect decisions. They all have some pluses and some minuses. For someone who is not good at making decisions the simplest first step is to make out a plus and minus column and look at what you fill in. This is a very useful thing for couples to do when faced with a big joint decision. Moving house has costs and benefits. They may be different for each partner, but by writing them down in an easy to compare manner partners can discuss the weight of the various options in a comprehensive way and greatly increase the chances of both people being comfortable with the choice that is made.

A good decision-maker knows that the downside of the decision made often affects people and that this negative fallout has to be acknowledged and managed. One person is promoted and others are not. There is always a reaction to a decision and one should not bury one's head in the sand and assume it will go away.

Do you ever find yourself telling someone you will 'think about it' when you already know that your answer will be 'no'? Why do you do it? Is it because you are not able to tell them the truth to their face? You are probably not doing them any favours by keeping whatever hope they have alive. You may even be wasting their time and stopping them getting on with something else.

A decision changes the psychological landscape, particularly if one has to decide between two equally attractive options. Sometimes a period of post-decision regret kicks in when the rejected option looks more desirable. But soon we start to see things that support our decision and strengthen the belief that we made the right decision. Watch it happen when you buy a car. The good decision-maker knows that this process will happen and takes it into account so as not to feel pressure to reverse what was probably a good decision in the first place.

Maybe the best model is what the Brian Kerrs of the world have to do. They pick the team, make the substitutions, explain their actions, take the flak, and start all over again. You may not like all the decisions, but imagine what it would be like if they weren't sure which way to go and had that indecisive look on their face. Football managers do not know great job security, but any sign of indecision and they wouldn't last five minutes.

So if you are a decision-maker who is clogging up the system then please get off the fence and it will be greatly appreciated by those around you – if all else fails, toss a coin.

Fighting and flirting — the Christmas party

Ooooooh Nooooo. Why did I do that? Or why did I say that? Worse still, did I really do that? Yep. Christmas comes but once a year. Too much affection. Too much aggression. Lurking in the background the culprit – too much alcohol. The wheels get oiled and then the wheels come off. After 'Happy Christmas' and 'Happy New Year', the most frequent phrase you hear that time of the year is 'Never Again'.

People have worked hard all year and deserve a bit of a blast. All through the year whatever sexual chemistry is around the office, well most of it, is happily contained by jokes and a bit of flirting. Then there is the office party. There is an element of the film world about office parties. The old phrase 'it doesn't count on location', used to excuse many away from home amorous clinches, applies. There is no need to rush home and tell the person's partner that they let themselves down. It could be your turn one day. Everybody, and that means everybody, should have the decency to forget what happened. Another old rule also applies. Don't expect your partner to understand.

There are two things to remember. One, don't do it and two, whoever organises the party should make sure that cameras are banned, because under the lens even the most innocent clinch after a few drinks looks like a lascivious leer and you don't want to look back at it. Ever. If somebody tells you it was only a peck on the cheek you were guilty of you can conservatively assume it was a five-minute clinch. You are forewarned.

But irrespective of misdemeanours, Christmas is a time for high tension as well as enjoyment. There is scarcely a family in the country that will not suffer the bad temper spilling over into a row. Why is that and what can be done to prevent it?

A lot of it comes down to space and giving people some. At Christmas, there are times when it is hard to find a chair to sit down on in your own house. When friends and neighbours are gone, there are usually relatives there overnight. You are either a guest or you have guests. The mantra you should have on your mind all the way through Christmas is not 'am I getting enough space?', but 'am I giving enough space?'

Our lives are a mixture of routine and excitement and for most of the year there is equilibrium between the two. We need routine to give us the stability against which to enjoy the excitement. At Christmas we often do not get enough routine and the result is that we become a bit short tempered. Things that we would normally shrug off come more frequently and then one of them tips the balance and we say something we will regret.

Watch for it in others and be ready to back off a bit. But more importantly, watch for it in yourself. If you feel the tension rising make yourself scarce for a while, because if you are feeling the heat, rest assured someone else is too and they may have a lot more on their plate than you do.

We love our brothers, sisters, uncles, aunts, etc. Well, maybe not all of them. But in many cases, we love our friends a lot more. Or at least we find them easier to get on with. So, try to treat your relations more like friends, and count to ten if they don't come up to the mark.

Just try to be a bit thoughtful. Christmas is a time when many people feel the sadness of remembering loved ones no longer with us. Amidst all the fuss and bother that brings a meaning to Christmas that people of all faiths and none can understand. Some people are special to us. So let's be nice to them. Some people aren't special to us. Let's try harder.

Going offside? No, just emotional infidelity

Are you one of those happily married people who looks forward to going to work on Monday to have a cup of coffee and a heart to heart with your close friend at work? Close friend of the opposite sex, that is. If so, you had better watch out, if you value your happy marriage. A Miami Beach psychologist, M. Gary Neuman, caused something of a stir when he published a book titled *Emotional Infidelity*, a book that decries male-female relationships outside marriage as a form of adultery. But while many in the marriage guidance field thought he was taking it a bit far, all were quick to admit that there was something in his central point – that friendships between members of the opposite sex can harm marriages.

Neuman believes that 'we can't fool ourselves into believing that we can have intimate relationships at work and still have great relationships at home ... If you want to infuse passion and have a buddy for the rest of your life, you have to keep the emotional content in your marriage'. The key concept is that this is happening all the time with people who are not looking for affairs and have good marriages. But they unwittingly cross the line forming deep passionate relationships before they even realise that they have moved from the platonic to the romantic. Such are the social changes of the workplace that relationships impossible a generation ago are commonplace now. It has huge consequences for women who work. In the US the divorce rate is 40% higher for working than non-working women.

Various researchers have concluded that about one-quarter of wives and almost half of husbands have had extra-marital sex. For almost two-thirds of the men and half the women, it was with someone at work. Because such a high proportion of the population has extensive pre-marital sexual experiences, it is not so great a taboo to have sex again after marriage. But for those forming intimate, opposite-sex friendships where it does not go as far as full intercourse it is thought that the overall figure is almost three-quarters.

In many of these cases, it is handled well by all concerned. But this intimacy crosses into the harmful 'emotional affair' when three things begin to happen – the person begins to share more of their inner highs and lows with the friend than with the spouse. Next, an element of secrecy creeps in and they would not admit the frequency of the meetings to the partner, and finally there is some chemistry even if not acted upon.

Put these things together and the real partner begins to feel frozen out. Trust is being betrayed. So, what is the best way to keep emotional intimacy in the home rather than the office? An easy step is to make sure that you as a couple have time each week where meaningful conversation can and does happen. Many couples get so involved in the project of 'the children' that they do not make time to nurture their own relationship and end up having chats with someone outside the marriage instead. Showing the commitment and giving attention within the marriage is the oxygen that keeps the love alive.

People need to set boundaries, and keep in mind that a relationship that is not fed with emotional intimacy is a dying one. Monogamy is not a natural state for human beings. It is a choice people make and like any choice it has consequences about how they behave. At the office, be careful of the heart to hearts. Watch it if you always have coffee and/or lunch with the same opposite sex co-worker. Don't meet them alone outside work. Celebrate successes with the whole group. Be careful about the amount of personal conversation you have because it will just begin to replace the personal conversations you should be having at home. If your conversation becomes peppered with sexual innuendo then you are moving it along. Remember that every time you touch somebody your relationship becomes more intimate and you go one step closer to crossing a line that you never contemplated in the early stages. If drink is involved, be 10 times more vigilant. Don't allow yourself to fantasise about the friend, because thoughts lead to actions.

Remember that the more attractive you find somebody the more careful you need to be. Above all, remember that the trouble has started long before the physical intimacy line even comes into view.

Bullying – just say 'no'

Where does strong management end and bullying begin? Not an easy question to answer. What is the difference between running a tight ship and ending up like Captain Blyth?

Part of the difference is history. Things that were accepted in the past are no longer considered appropriate. This is the case with regard to how employers treat employees, how managers deal with staff, and, with the workplace now comprising almost equal numbers of men and women, how the sexes communicate with each other in the work environment.

Bullies make demands on people, they control them as much as they can, they often have considerable difficulty in seeing another person's point of view, show contempt for other people's feeling, dish out verbal abuse, and rate their own needs above all others. I can think of one person I had the dubious pleasure of watching in operation in my distant past who got great satisfaction out of using the phone on a whim to make people hop to attention and run around in circles. I can still see the satisfied look on that face after the phone was put down and I am sure the same facial muscles had been in use since that same person pocketed all the marbles in the playground.

Bullies are formed in childhood and they keep doing it as long as it works for them. There is some evidence that punitive treatment of children makes them emotionally colder. They then show less empathy for their victim and the situation is further complicated because the aggressive parents who produce these children reward them for dominance.

The rest of us are not entirely innocent. Who cannot remember a childhood scene when we let it happen, glad it wasn't happening to us? We may have even convinced ourselves that the unfortunate victims deserved all they got. Adults often were not much help. I have clear memories of teachers stopping a fight, and then using the same nickname to torture the unfortunate person at the bottom of the pile.

Bullies are often insecure and jealous of those around them. Someone else's ability or talent or popularity can serve as a trigger to get them started. It is not unusual for bullies to surround themselves with far weaker people who will not challenge them. Paradoxically this can often result in the bully shining by comparison with the others and being promoted. This furthers their misplaced sense of superiority and lessens their concern for others even more.

Wherever there is power it will be abused. In the old days of a rigidly structured factory set-up bullying was probably approved of, or even rewarded, by a happy employer. Today work is more voluntary and creativity, loyalty, self-starting, and commitment are far more important than compliant behaviour. But creativity, confidence and growth of talent are the very things that die in a bullying atmosphere.

Bullying can take many forms. Rumours can be spread. Not just the bully socially isolates the victim, but also others who are caught up in the gossip. The 'feel good' atmosphere is the first thing to vanish.

Some of the effects of being bullied are similar to Post Traumatic Stress Disorder. The victim may feel moody and guilty. They are likely to suffer nightmares, have difficulty falling asleep, be irritable, have poor concentration, and have an exaggerated startle response where a small fright makes them almost jump out of their skin.

The signs of the bullying personality to keep an eye out for? They are usually, but not always, male, typically between 30 and 40, often socially isolated, and may have an unstable family life. They may show evidence of poor self-esteem, have problems controlling their anger, regularly complain about work conditions, and be full of perceived injustices that they have suffered.

Inevitably, some people tolerate things that others among us wouldn't countenance for five minutes. So, what is it that turns some people into 'victims'?

Q: What does a bully look for?
A: A submissive person.

What is it that makes some people targets, while others would not come into the sights of even the nastiest of bullies? If you are in the unfortunate position of suffering abuse what is the best way to deal with it?

Bullying has been defined as the systematic abuse of power, and one important part of the system is the selection of a suitable victim. Research on children shows that up to the age of seven bullies pick on anyone. After that age, they pick on particular children as victims. Targeted children tend to be the more sensitive, quiet and cautious children. These young people do not like conflict and will go a long way to avoid confrontation. They do not have good conflict resolution skills and frequently give the bully what they want. It could be a favourite toy but they will part with it and as if to throw in a bonus, they are likely to cry. So, the bully gets by far the biggest rewards from someone with those qualities.

The children who are bullied tend to be passive, often play alone, are not good at starting conversations with the result that they are not particularly popular with the non-bullying children either, so do not have natural allies to defend them. Interestingly, the child is father of the man. The signs are that those children retain the 'whipping boy' status for the rest of their life in many cases.

An adult who becomes the subject of bullying at work will ask 'why me?' But while they may be surprised it is happening to them, if they look back they will see a pattern. The central problem, whether as child or adult, is that they lack the skills to assert themselves against the dominant people.

The term 'harassment' is often used to describe the more psychological forms of aggression that cause stress in the workplace. We have all seen the person who takes pleasure out of ridiculing a colleague in front of others. What did we do? We probably laughed. The harasser may claim it a 'just a bit of fun', not realising the impact it is having.

That it is the weak who are targeted is clear in the people selected for phone-call harassment which will be typically threatening and sexual in nature. The unfortunate women are far more likely to be divorced, separated or very young.

The middle manager who delights in pushing people around can make a person's life miserable. But if they go so far as to complain, often the victim is not taken seriously. Part of the problem is that senior managers are not the type of people who have ever been bullied and so find it hard to believe it is happening. They think it is just the lazy person being given a much needed push. This is compounded if the bully also happens to have the get up and go that they admire in an employee.

We are all entitled to feel as secure in work as we do at home, to feel valued and respected as people and not just for the job performed. It is the task of good management to create this climate.

The best defence against being a victim for life is to develop a more assertive way of dealing with people. When criticised ask for further explanation. There often is none because the bully was just trying to hurt, not to be accurate.

Bounce bullying comments straight back at them. People are often shocked to hear what they sound like. Keep coming back to the point. The bully will bluff and bluster all over the place to dominate you, but if you keep coming back to the one point at issue they will have to deal with it sooner or later. If this happens in public, they are unlikely to pick on you again.

Get your body language right. Think confident even if you are quaking. Most of the meaning is carried not in the words, but in the way we deliver them. There is no point in talking like an Alsatian while looking like a poodle!

A friend in need?

You can become friends with your boss, but what happens if one of your friends becomes your boss. This is a dilemma for all involved and one that is becoming increasingly common as we no longer look to family to give that feeling of closeness that comes with knowing another person intimately. An important part of friendship is that it is reciprocal with each person meshing with the needs of the other to give a feeling of well-being during much of the time spent together. Now the personal dynamics at work and at the weekend are going to have to change, and how much of a battering they take depends on many factors.

There was a time when you could predict every promotion in places like the army, civil service and many large established companies with near certainty. There was an established order and it threw up few surprises.

Workplaces today are a great deal more open than a generation ago. People use first names a lot more. If tasks are well defined and carried out competently there is opportunity for work to be a socially pleasant place. More of one's personality gets involved in the working hours and less of a rigid role is required by the job. Real people get to know real people, discover they share a sense of humour, and frequently these relationships spill over outside the office. The transition from acquaintance to friend happens – so meals out, concerts at Slane, mountains climbed, even holidays take place with the gang from work.

That is fine and dandy until somebody's status changes. Suddenly you have to report to your friend, and cope with them having more money and status that you might have had an eye on yourself. So how do you manage the situation if you want to preserve the friendship and get on with the job? Friendships change with our lives. Some strengthen, and some will fizzle out and vanish. But a central part of friendship is that feeling of knowing the other person. The new situation will interfere with that sense of knowing. So there may be gaps that have to be replaced to maintain the feeling of closeness.

It may be worth the effort. Samuel Butler observed that friendship is like money, easier made than kept.

Maybe you all knew that a job was up for grabs and several of you went for it. Then it is best to be open with each other and decide in advance that whoever the lucky one is, you will all celebrate.

Try to put yourself in the other's shoes. If nothing else, this helps people avoid saying the wrong thing. Realise that a job change brings stress as well as rewards to the friend and they could probably do with some support. In particular, they don't want their social life to go pear-shaped at a time of good fortune.

But the new boss also has to realise that their friends' egos will be a bit dented, even if they didn't apply for or want the job. Even the most mature and well-balanced view themselves in relation to their peers and while being pleased about another's success this is also a time for doubts about their own place in life to surface. In a world where people tend to define themselves by their job, they may worry that they will be taken less seriously both at work and outside.

Everyone needs to watch for the vipers in the company looking for an opportunity to exploit the change in the *status quo*. They will be only too happy to point out the unfairness of the new situation, real or imagined. There is always the rebel looking to form a divisive subgroup. They thrive at times like this.

Whatever the feelings people should not vent them in public. Particularly if there is any danger of alcohol doing the talking for you! All should avoid getting into a situation where jealousy and resentment can surface.

Keep talking, because communication is vital. When interacting at work, be professional. When in a social situation be friendly, but everyone involved needs to realise that the script has changed a bit, particularly at work.

Maybe you will have to leave work more at work. Put a glass wall there, and perhaps there will be enough in the friendship to shift a gear for the sake of all concerned.

If not, then start looking for another job!

The right personality for the job

One of our neighbours always took a kindly interest in my school results. It was clear that maths was my best subject. Now this man was also a successful businessman who knew which way the wind was blowing. 'Accountancy,' he said, 'was the coming thing'. But I was more interested in living inside a set of headphones, and being fired up with 'the times, they are a changin'.'

He was right about accountancy. But wrong that it was for me. I may have been good at sums, but my personality was wrong for the job. I might be driving a top of the range Merc now, but I would also probably be swallowing anti-depressants, or worse. It used to be thought that intelligence was the most important predictor of how well someone would do at work, or indeed life. But clearly people are more complicated than that and we now recognise that it is a blend of intellectual ability and personality that matters – and personality is probably the more important. I don't mean any particular personality, not everyone needs to be a live wire. But a personality suited to what you will be doing every day in the job.

Just which personality traits predict successful performance in a job? Psychologists have identified five important traits and different ones are more influential depending on the job.

Extroversion – the extent to which a person is sociable and out-going, and perhaps impulsive. Fun to be with, and with a whiff of danger.

Neuroticism – is the person tense and do they tend to worry? About everything. Even when there is no apparent need. These people are the bread and butter of psychotherapy.

Three more traits are increasingly being seen as the ones that count. Firstly, *openness*. This is the extent to which one is flexible and positive towards new experiences. Think Michael O'Leary. This is the vital ingredient for creativity. And when you look at how much people fear change you realise it is a rare enough commodity.

Agreeableness – being warm and good-natured towards others. In a less rigidly hierarchical world, the ability to get on with people while working at something together is increasingly valuable. Think

Bertie Ahern, but then he is also well equipped with the other important qualities.

Finally *conscientiousness* – being organised, responsible, and determined to achieve goals and deadlines. This seems to be the most important ingredient for success in a wide range of jobs from the manual to the managerial. This is what you want in your surgeon as you contemplate eternity. But it doesn't work where you want creativity, because it is one of those quirks of nature that creative people are less likely to be organised and responsible.

One American study found that the most successful musicians in the eyes of other musicians had the lowest scores on being conscientious. Now that doesn't mean they aren't determined to succeed or that they are lazy. I'm sure U2 spend more time in the studio than many MDs do in the office. They probably even work to deadlines, but with a different attitude. Maybe this is why rock groups have managers.

People skills are the glue that holds it all together. You may be introverted, but if you have good interpersonal skills you can muster enough get up and go to address a meeting. Or a naturally aggressive person can keep it under control and present himself or herself as charming. As more and more jobs involve working with people and dealing with the public these skills are hugely valuable. Imagine a world where you asked a question in the supermarket and didn't get the 'not my aisle' blank stare of unhelpfulness!

Personality is also now being seen as vital to predicting how the person performs on things peripheral to the job itself – the people who volunteer, who put in the extra effort with a smile. Think of the teachers who do the games and put on the school play, versus the ones that are in the car park five minutes after the bell rings and you'll know what I mean.

Losing the head

I can't stand people who lose their temper. I never could. I think it was just stamped out of us in school where it was branded childish. But a bit of healthy anger – that is a different thing. You feel a lot better for it, and it does make people sit up and take notice.

Social psychologists have shown that high status people are more likely to feel anger. They have more to be happy about, and they have more to be angry about. They also have greater freedom in the emotions they are allowed to express in public than those lower down the pecking order.

But recent research suggests that this is a two-way street and that people who express anger are perceived as deserving of status, more knowledgeable and, consequently, they are more likely to be promoted. Does this have a ring of truth? We have all seen the big-mouth singled out for praise and advancement, while the worker bees who regularly cleared up the mess the 'jerk' created, and who were far more entitled to promotion, were overlooked. They were probably more capable to boot. Hiding your light under a bushel does not seem to be a good strategy.

Anger in an office is one of those things where a little can go a long way. Think of the person who loses the head and shouts down the phone. Workmates give them a wide berth. Those at the receiving end hold the phone away from their ear if they have any sense. The person who frequently loses their temper is unpleasant to be around and is best not being tolerated. A workplace where people have to tread on eggshells is not a productive place to be.

But there are situations where the expression of anger can make a good impression. It can show that the person really cares about a shared aim. The person is blowing their top, but not at their workmates.

The issue of looking in control is central. Out of character behaviour is seen, wrongly as it happens, as being far more revealing about a person's personality than all of the hours of consistent, routine, predictable behaviour. One day at work with blue hair, or a nose stud, will be talked about for years. But it won't get you taken seriously. A more effective way to stand out from the crowd may be to give rein to some of your feelings.

If people are displaying anger about something important to the company they are seen positively, and active and strong traits are more likely to be rewarded by promotion than passivity and weakness. People who make decisions about hiring and promoting are often not aware of the biases they bring to the task. It is the more dynamic behaviour that will stick in their minds.

Politicians are one group who know all about perception. For them it is often not about telling the story. It is about what will look good. In one recent American study people were shown two edited version of Bill Clinton dealing with the Monica Lewinsky affair. In one version, clips of him speaking contritely were shown. In the other, he responded angrily. The people who viewed the angry Clinton were much more likely to believe that he should remain president. They may not have liked what he did, but the angry portrayal inferred the type of qualities they believed a president should have.

There is a world of difference between losing one's temper and displaying controlled anger. It is the difference between a very hard tackle and a red card. The display of controlled anger is all the more impressive in one who uses it very sparingly.

It is not that blowing your top helps you make it to the top, more that if you really care your normal calm will break down on occasion. Provided you don't lash out unfairly at those in the vicinity, the decision-makers just might be impressed. It might be the first time they notice you are a bit of a bright spark.

Office romance - tread carefully

You have to meet somebody to fall in love with them and it helps if you share interests. So it is hardly surprising that teachers often fall in love with teachers, gardaí fall in love with ban gardaí, athletes marry their coaches, and lawyers love lawyers.

Think of 20 couples you know. Where did they meet? I think you will find that a lot of them met through work. Almost everybody can think of a romance at work and that is not surprising as almost half of all romantic relationships begin at work. Today work is a far more reliable source of a mate than pubs, night clubs or your local walking club. About one quarter of all marriages are between people who met at work. No wonder that some commentators are referring to the office as the hottest singles scene around. As one slightly cynical American put it – 'Dating somebody at the office certainly makes work more interesting'!

Most of us have seen that frisson develop between people at work. It is in the body language, the tone of voice on the phone, a look, and we sense that two people who were colleagues have moved a stage further. Here is a sobering statistic – more than half of all men admit to having had sex with someone at work. Now it doesn't take a genius to work out many of these men are married, and not to the person at work!

There are lots of good reasons why love is flourishing at work. People now marry later so there are more single people around. Increasingly marriages break up so there are people of all ages ready for a relationship. With more women working the sex ratio is much closer to 50–50.

The workplace is also a more sexualised environment. You may slob around the house in sweatshirt and tracksuit bottoms, but people go to work groomed to perfection. By any criteria people look a lot more fanciable than in the days when your work suit only saw the dry cleaners twice a year and hemlines were lower.

But is a marriage that has its roots in the nine to five part of the day likely to fare any better than one that begins with a nightclub grope in the small hours of the morning? There are a number of reasons why working together in the early days may just keep you loving together. It all comes down to the time spent together in a range of situations that give you a chance to get to know the other person without hormones clouding judgement.

At work, you are less likely to make a snap judgement. We probably decide we fancy someone in a fraction of a second. Along with this lust go a large number of assumptions we make about that person's personality, most of which will turn out to be wrong. But in the workplace, you see many facets of the person's behaviour so are likely to form a more real picture of the prospective partner. You are also more likely to take your time and anything that holds us back a bit cannot be bad. As a generalisation, a short courtship is a good predictor of a short marriage!

Add to that the likelihood that people in the same line of work will share interests and attitudes, and then the killer application of the workplace – propinquity – people are physically near to each other. Long hours are spent together and familiarity does not necessarily breed contempt. Knowing each other can happen at a natural pace. You don't have to make up your mind by 'last drinks'. Crucially for women, work is seen as a safe environment.

For co-workers the problems begin when the romance is carried on a bit too much in public. You can fight over the cornflakes but don't bring the atmosphere past the office door. There is no need to make up at the photocopier. Another problem is specific to romance between a superior and a subordinate. Colleagues will see favouritism, whether real or imagined. Then there is the nightmare for everybody when the couple decide to break up, and one or other seeks revenge or seeks to rekindle, but in either case force everyone to get involved in their own personal soap opera.

Concerns such as these have prompted many companies to try to ban romance in the office, or at least monitor it. Some large companies are now insisting that daters should inform their human resources department of their relationship and even sign a 'consensual relationship contract policy' which indemnifies the company against legal action. Now there is a way to get off to a good start – half a glass of Moët and 'sign here please'. I suppose you could think of it as a dry run for the pre-nup! Office romances between all combinations of ages, sexes and marital status have gone on for as long as people have been working together so management have an uphill battle if they want to ban it.

Peoples' definitions of love are quite idiosyncratic. Ask the five people nearest to you what 'being in love' means to them and you will be surprised at the differences. The work environment is not conducive to mad passion (well, between nine and five anyway) and all the evidence is that more pragmatic and less high octane love has a greater chance of lasting. Women are more inclined to favour this kind of relationship, but they are becoming more like men!

One American survey in the 1960s asked men and women the question 'If a person had all the qualities you desired but you didn't love them would you still marry them?' Two-thirds of men said 'no', but only a quarter of the women. By the 1980s, both had changed to over 80% saying 'no'. We all want more romance.

Similarity is attractive. It is well known that relationships where the couple enjoy a wide range of activities together have a better prognosis than those who do less together. What is crucial about the time spent together is that the couple develop the feeling of intimacy that comes from sharing deeply personal ideas and feelings. At the centre of it all is communication, which is something the modern man is still not good at. But work is something that men *can* talk about, even be emotional about.

At work, you have to be a better listener than you might get away with at home. You have to actively listen, instead of thinking about what you are going to say next. Active listening enables you to check if you have really understood the other person. With a workmate, it makes for smooth relationships. With a workmate who is a lover, feeling really listened to increases intimacy – particularly if the habit carries over to the home.

The demands of the working environment mean that people must be civil to each other most of the time. You just cannot lose the head and slam doors the way one might at home. Nor can one sulk at length. Working together can enhance developing the skills to resolve conflict. A delay of as little as five seconds at the beginning of a disagreement, biting one's tongue, hugely increases the chances of solving a problem without raised voices. Incidentally, in good marriages the positivity to negativity ratio is about 5:1. In bad marriages, about 1:1.

How do people manage the early stages when they don't want everyone in the canteen to know that they were walking the Wicklow hills over the weekend and, well, one thing lead to another? Confidentiality can create a strong bond.

The next step is to make commitment and go public. Typically, couples relax standards at this stage and become less careful about how they treat each other. If they are still working together, they cannot let this happen.

The evidence is that if a relationship is going to break down then around 15 to 18 months is a vulnerable time because by then they know enough about each other to know if it is going to work out – and not all do. This is, of course, hell for everyone in the vicinity.

Finally, three-quarters of men admit to fantasising about a colleague. One wonders what the figure for women is. Nothing wrong with looking at what is on the menu, I suppose. Eating gives you those stomach-churning experiences. So, tread carefully. The workplace is a good place to find a long-term mate. But spare a thought for your colleagues if you are the flighty type. They don't need a new drama every few weeks!

Negotiate, don't fight

Conflict is a feature of our lives every day. While some people are always spoiling for a fight most of us would rather resolve our differences without raised voices and name-calling. Not least because many of the relationships we have at home and at work are ongoing. To live in a constant state of tension is not very pleasant.

When we differ with other people there are a few common mistakes that can make a bad situation worse, and a few simple rules can help us get what we want without causing mayhem. Like it or not we negotiate all of the time because most of the time our interests and the interests of others around us are not exactly the same. So even if you both want to see *The Gangs of New York* this week you may not agree on which day, which cinema, whether to have a meal before, or a drink after, not earth-shattering decisions in a highly charged competitive atmosphere, but negotiations all the same. You soon become aware of this if one person always decides and never compromises.

The Harvard University Negotiation Project has studied disputes ranging from those between the world powers to those in the home and has concluded that there are three features found in a good negotiation. The result will be *wise*, and by that they mean an agreement that is fair and durable and meets everyone's interests as far as possible. It will be *efficient*. That is, you will not be worn to a frazzle by the time you agree. Most importantly, it should *improve*, or at the very least not damage, the relationship between the people involved. There is no point in making enemies in a world where we all need friends.

For many people there are only two kinds of negotiation – hard and soft. The negotiation becomes a battle of wills as each side states and defends their position. The hard negotiator takes an extreme position and refuses to budge. They will mislead about their bottom line. They will often adopt a 'take it or leave it' attitude and wear the opponent down. This is the tactic of bullies and the agreement that is reached does not meet any of the above criteria.

The soft negotiator is up front about their bottom line and concerned about the personal relationship and not causing conflict. In the battle of wills, they reach agreement but again it is not a good one because they were too concerned about the personal emotions and feelings about which their opponent cares not one jot.

One way out of this impasse is to change the rules. There is no need for a bottom line and the struggle is not between people and their positions. It is a problem to be solved taking into account the legitimate interests of each side. As far as possible, some objective criteria can be brought to bear. Two people may be getting nowhere about the price of a car. One says €7,000. The other says €9,000 and they are like two gunfighters at the OK corral. But if they agree to decide to work through how much the air conditioning is worth, how much the low mileage matters, and the CD player, and leather seats, and the age of the car they are quickly into more objective criteria and movement to an agreement becomes possible. Often when you see it as a solvable problem creative ways of finding options for your mutual benefit begin to emerge.

But remember, you are always dealing with another person and that person has emotions and values just as you have. The more you are able to see the situation from their side the better a negotiator you are likely to be.

Brainstorm the negotiation with friends and colleagues before you embark on it. Then do the hard bit. Brainstorm it from the other side, with their emotions, values and what face they have to gain or lose in mind.

When face-to-face it is sometimes useful to summarise how you feel. It is always hard for someone to challenge you about what you feel because you have all the evidence. They may tell you they don't care how you feel but then at least you know where you stand – and where to walk.

Timing is everything

Timing is everything, whether you are talking about your golf swing, when to ask your parents for more pocket money, or when to ask your boss for a raise or a change in working arrangements. In short if you want to ask anybody to do something that they may not be keen on doing, when you raise the question has a big influence on whether you get what you want or not. When you want to change another person's behaviour, whether senior, junior or at the same level as you, it helps to get a good understanding of their routines, habits and personalities. Whether we like to think so or not human beings are very predictable animals and things in our diary get set in stone, transferring automatically from one week to the next. So if your line manager has a tension filled group meeting each Wednesday at 11 then you know not to make your pitch full of the joys of spring in the canteen half an hour earlier. At best, you will get a 'come back to me about that later' and that is not a good start – ever!

We all have a routine about how we behave at work. We tend to feel best when it is going smoothly. That is why people get so irritated about being caught in traffic and arriving 20 minutes late. They often complain about feeling behind and playing catch up for the rest of the day. For some people getting off to that bad start has a negative effect on the rest of the day. We are all familiar with people who would rather be a half an hour early than five minutes late because they know the effect it has on them.

People can become quite crotchety when routines are upset. We think through what we expect to do during the day and then get quite perturbed when someone doesn't turn up for something crucial so vital items are postponed. It is that same feeling that we get when we stay in all morning because the plumber has promised to come. By mid-day you are extremely angry and will not be in your most flexible, approachable, mood.

Of course, it is not the same for everybody. We all have our own personality to bring to the mishaps of the day. Some just shrug off what will drive another person to distraction. One person is upset for days because their team loses a crucial match. Another is disappointed with the result and moves on to next week, or year. But the more we know about another person's personality the more we are able to pick our best time to find them receptive to our request.

Some people are now saying that a larger thing also comes into play as well as individual routine and personality and that is the structure of the Monday to Friday week that the majority of people still work. In psychological terms, not every day is the same. You can immediately picture your typical Monday and you don't have to think long to know why Bob Geldof had a hit. You have just had two relaxed days when you could do what you liked and you are back to the pressure. In today's Ireland you are surrounded with too many people still a touch hungover! Monday is a hard day because everyone takes off from a standing start to get the week organised with goals being set and reality is back big time. Even people who love their jobs love Monday a lot less. Everybody is trying to get everybody moving again.

A lot is done on Tuesday and Wednesday and unpleasantness peaks for many people by the end of Wednesday by which time they have had to deal with too much hassle and the weekend is still a long time away. Thursday brings a big change in attitude because they have done enough to look back on the week, hopefully with a good number of boxes ticked, the weekend plans have been made and it is just around the corner. It is also payday for a lot of people.

Finally, Friday is the day that most people are a push-over. It is not a coincidence that Friday was the day companies chose for dressing casually. It wouldn't have worked on Monday. So when are people their most flexible? Well towards the end of the week, all things being equal, is the time when people have the space to be more flexible, compromising and open to new ideas.

8

Slings & Arrows

Giving out lemon drops

Is there anyone out there who can honestly say they don't mind being criticised? That it doesn't hurt. Sometimes more than others.

There are the small barbs, often unintentional. I smile when I remember a thank you card I received from a weekend guest many years back telling me she thought my house 'had great potential'. I had thought my house was finished to perfection at the time and felt like wringing her neck. Momentarily. Then sense of humour came to the rescue. With the bonus of having a story to tell at her expense.

As an undergraduate, I did three years of Philosophy at Trinity College. A major component of the course was the tutorial, a small group of four or five students and lone lecturer. One of us would be invited to read our essay aloud and it would be then ripped to shreds, mercilessly, by all present. Ideas were discussed, dissected, disputed as things with their own life, entirely separate from the poor person who had just suggested them. In this cauldron we built up a very high tolerance for accepting criticism, learned how to defend our ideas and not to take things personally.

Unfortunately, we also learned how to dish it out very effectively. No one ever mentioned to us that other people might not relish having the ground ripped out from under them. So we scratched our heads and muttered 'What's wrong with him. I only said he was talking rubbish?' On we went with that undergraduate arrogance. I remember happily pointing out their shortcomings to my parents and being slightly taken aback that they didn't appreciate my taking the time to share my educational benefits, which they were paying for, with them!

Sadly, people who are good at dishing the dirt learn to get hurt about a decade before they learn to stop hurting. We are able to feel sorry for ourselves long before we can feel the hurt we might cause in others. The simple maxim to do unto others as you would like them to do to you takes a while to sink in.

So, in work, as in life, most people struggle with the art of telling people unpleasant things about themselves. From dealing with the person who consistently turns up late to the person who is close to losing their job if they do not change, we cannot avoid dishing out lemon drops. But we can lessen the pain and increase the effectiveness.

First, try a variant of hating the sin but not the sinner. It is important to point out not only what is wrong but what can be done about it. Give the person room to move, and a clear idea of the direction in which they should be moving. By focusing on the behaviour, you keep away from the global treatment of the person as 'a lazy person' or 'a careless person'. Instead, they are a fine person and you would like to see some changes which you can specify, and give a reason for. Setbacks are then seen as due to circumstances we can do something about. They are not a personal failing.

People often do not need to be criticised. They are already doing it to themselves. In my first job, a very short foray into market research, I made a massive mistake as I said earlier. I went to the head of the company to explain what had happened, confidently expecting a tirade, and probably to be fired as well. He listened carefully. Then said something along the lines that it was the last time I would make that mistake, before adding that 'in his experience the only people who didn't make mistakes were the people who weren't doing very much'. Effective management.

Contrast that with those appalling people who can only react to an apology by rubbing your nose in it for a while. Or the boss who goes over your mistake repeatedly, having forgotten that it was you who told him about it!

Before you decide to criticise, try to imagine how the other person will react to what you are going to say and then think about whether there is a better away to achieve your goal.

It is always worth looking at what Ambrose Bierce, in his Devil's Dictionary, said at times like this – come down off your high horse. He defined a critic as someone 'who boasts himself hard to please because nobody tries to please him'.

Rejected again - the power of SORRY

If I am to do something new this year I am sure that it will be to spend more time on the net. Up to now, I would send and check my e-mails and look for things that I needed to know. I would book the odd plane ticket or buy a CD. But it was just an adjunct to my normal life. Not at the centre of it. No more.

I spent Christmas with a computer that was on line 24 hours a day, 7 days a week. That changes everything because you begin to browse. For every blind alley you go up, there is another one with a little gem at the end. My find this week was www.rejectioncollection.com with its suggestion of how to deal with rejection through a five-step plan called SORRY. This site comes with a sense of humour attached which is no bad thing if feeling a bit low. So if you have ever not got the job you desperately needed (and are sure you deserved), been unceremoniously dumped by a loved one, or not been picked for the trip.

Here are the vital ingredients, of the SORRY programme for recovery:

S is for sob, but why stop there. Crying may be better, and if you are in a secure place why not have some full-blown rage and shout at the wall. You are entitled to it. Those fools, or that fool, do not know what they are missing and they needn't think they are going to come across the likes of you again. Boy, have they made a big mistake! If any of them ever cross your path, you won't get mad. But you will get even.

O is for obsess. It would have been the perfect job. Think about the company car, the status, the beautiful office with the flowers changed daily, maybe the occasional foreign trip. It was just the job for you. Your name on the door. The stylish business cards. The Christmas party where you would have shone. But you won't be there. All the other people will. Time for the green-eyed monster. Yes, if you really wanted that job you are jealous of them. If you really loved that person of course you are jealous of whoever, real or imagined, is now enjoying their company. Yep. This is the down part of SORRY. Feel the loss, and then get ready to face up to it.

R is for rant, and in my book it is also the beginning of reco-very. You have had the hissy fit in 'S'. This is a more focused rant. You may tell your best friend, again, about all the injustices you have suffered. But remember this is a currency that devalues very quickly and you could find yourself friendless, as well as jobless and loveless. No, far better that you put it down on paper, and that forces you to think it through. Lo and behold, some focus on the future, rather than the past, begins to emerge. You can even send your musings to www.rejectioncollection.com where it will remain anonymous and you can see that your misery has company.

R again and this one is for renew, regenerate, and remember the good things about yourself. This is a setback, but there are plenty of good things in life for you. Time to say goodbye to the re-grets and begin to feel good about yourself again. Make a list of times you felt proud of yourself, and the things you are good at. Don't be modest.

Finally **Y** is for yearn. Yes. You are looking forward again. This is the time to set the goals again. What is it that you want? How are you going to go about achieving that?

You are well on your way and already clouds have silver lin-ings. Onwards and upwards. 'To the toppermost of the popper-most', as John Lennon used to say.

A gun to your head - take a walk

I had a phone call from a friend a few weeks ago and to say the least he was a bit frazzled. This is a person who normally takes things in his stride, so what, I wondered, had unsettled him. It wasn't the first time I had heard the story.

Buying a house is always stressful, and with a little effort, it seems that people can make it even more stressful than necessary. He had seen a house that he was humming and hawing about. There was a lot he liked about it. It was definitely better than any other he had seen. He could afford it comfortably which got rid of one of the big stresses. But it didn't face the right direction and that was the one negative.

So, as happens during the process he was spending a lot of quality time in conversation with an estate agent. He put in a bid. A rival pushed it up. The cycle continued towards the top of what he felt it was worth. Then he had a gun put to his head. 'The house is yours if you go to … NOW' and a figure of €5,000 more was specified. Otherwise, the Dutch auction could go on forever. He sweated for a few minutes and said 'yes'. Within 15 minutes, he knew he had made the wrong decision. The orientation of the house was going to gnaw at him forever. He decided to sleep on it.

By morning, he was sure he had made the wrong decision and rang to withdraw his offer only to receive the tongue-lashing of his life from the estate agent. This was what had upset him. Had he done the wrong thing? He had gone back on his word. He had let the person down and he was upset.

Let's look at what happened. Can you remember the last time you faced an ultimatum? How did you feel? What would you think if someone told you he had given his girlfriend until the weekend to decide if she was going to marry him or not? I know what I would think!

Sometimes deadlines have to be met and decisions made. The plane won't wait for you. But when we know the time-scale, we can work towards it. Sometimes we know the timing is arbitrary and at best we feel controlled and at worst bullied.

Of course, the estate agent was annoyed. His tactic was close to bullying and it had come unstuck. So he tried one more throw of the dice to see if he could rescue the situation. But by this time my friend's back was up. He said 'no' but felt guilt.

Wrong emotion. It might be the appropriate thing to feel if you have genuinely let someone down on a promise freely made and well intended. But if someone has backed you into a corner then self-preservation comes way before keeping your word.

If you are not being treated with the respect you deserve, then the other person gives up their right to your normal standards of behaviour.

So, if you feel a gun put to your head, smell a rat and walk if you can. Sometimes you cannot walk. It may be your boss at work that is making the demand. Then reach for your anti-bullying strategies. Repeat back their words to them so that they can hear clearly what is coming out of their mouths. This alone may make them modify their style. It might have even worked with my friend's estate agent.

Whenever you feel controlled there is one thing at risk – your self-respect. It is not something you should let go of. So, if you cannot change the situation, get out of it. It will always be worth it in the long run. They can't control you if you are no longer on the payroll.

Stress - it's not all bad

Stress. It is the new 'black' of emotional problems. It has pushed burnout down to No. 2 in the 'life is getting on top of me' charts. If I am to believe what I read the entire world is in urgent need of deep massage, aromatherapy, soft music and a general chill out if they are to survive the rigours of life. Now maybe I am odd but I cannot think of anything more stressful than aromatherapy and soft music. You would have to tie me down, or at least put on Sky News. Which only goes to show that different things stress different people, and we handle stress in our own peculiar ways.

There are certainly a lot more minor irritants around these days and their cumulative effect is stressful. There is traffic which doesn't move, meetings that start late, mobile phones from which there is no escape, there are the cries of 'where did I put my keys?' and the e-mails that you could live without. High on my current list is being in the company of texters. You are having a conversation, the phone goes beep, and then they have to reply immediately. To top it all a cappuccino now costs more than a beer, hell, even water costs as much as beer, and we all suspect the weather is gradually getting worse!

With the little things, we can decide not to let them get us down. Getting angry in the traffic will not make it move any faster so you may as well roll down the window and smell the roses. If someone is late for a meeting, you can change your mindset and do something useful for 10 minutes instead of fuming. But could we do the same with the bigger stresses? Can we turn the stress into something positive?

It depends to some degree on how we deal with stress and how severe the stress is. Some people feel more in control of their life than others and this helps them deal with problem situations. They see life as simple cause and effect and believe you can do something about your plight. If you are not getting through your work, then begin earlier. If you have difficulty at work, talk to the right person about it and get it sorted out. These people view life as a combination of circumstances and if they are not producing the right result they step in and change something. Find the source of stress and deal with it.

Others deal with stress in a more emotion-focused way. Rather than deal with the source of the stress they try to modify their reaction to the stress. Thus, they may tune out, or keep a stiff upper lip. This is the 'whenever I feel afraid, I whistle a happy tune' approach and it has its merits.

The difference between the two approaches comes down to what control one believes one has over the situation. There are times at work when you are swamped and you just have to grin and bear it. Think of the people who work in shops up to Christmas, get a few days off, and then face into the January sales. They couldn't work at that pace all year round, but when they know it is for a limited period, they gird their loins and get on with it.

The people who could get a lot more use out of stress are the ones who tend to take the emotional route without examining the 'let's see what I can do about this' route. Stress is not a pleasant feeling but it is going to be a feature of life whether we like it or not. So changing one's mindset to look for a solution may be the best way to reduce the stress and improve your quality of life in one action.

You cannot ignore long-term stress because it will eventually have damaging effects on your immune system and health. It is important to do something about it. So, take a good look and see what changes are possible.

You may be able to improve the situation. You may decide that nothing can be changed. If so, it is time to move on because if you don't deal with the stress, it will deal with you.

Having a perspective

Each Easter a small emotionally draining drama is played out as worried parents do their best to get teenagers to go to their rooms and do some study. The exams are not far away and offspring are being accused of not having done a tap all year. This is hotly denied by teenagers who know that in many cases there is more than a grain of truth in it.

The measure used to decide if the student can watch television or head off on the town is often the simplest one to count. 'How many hours have you done today?' I always listen to this conversation with a sinking heart because I was never one who could study for hours on end. If memory serves me correctly coming up to the exams I rarely did more than three hours a day and that was not one three-hour stint. It was three one-hour stints. After an hour, I was tired and beginning to get bored.

When I hear of people putting in massive sessions like eight hours in a day I wonder how effectively the time was spent. It immediately conjures up an image of a youth staring into space, playing with his or her hair, and having forgotten what was on page 34 by the time they begin page 35.

Effective study requires constantly checking to make sure you have understood what you have just applied your mind to. It requires memorising and being able to manipulate those memories in your head without the assistance of the words on the page. Then it requires taking a viewpoint about what is in your head, which is a more advanced skill. Consider a question like 'discuss Margaret Thatcher's handling of the Northern Ireland question'. You need more than names and dates to answer it. You need a perspective.

I am convinced that one hour reading with an attitude is far more useful that eight hours just ploughing through the chapters. To demonstrate take three people watching Spurs play Arsenal. One is an Arsenal supporter. One follows Manchester United and the third has no interest in football and barely knows the rules. At the end of the match, they each have to recall and assess the most

157

important aspects of the match and what changes should have been made to alter the result. It doesn't take much to know that their perspectives will affect what, and how much, is remembered. Think of the tallymen at an election who store vast amounts of data effortlessly because each vote matters to them.

Looking at something with an attitude forces us to categorise it and compare it with other information we already have. It is like doing non-stop revision. We test the information to see how well it fits our theory of the world and, to a degree, we test and change our theory as it fails to measure up.

Instead of counting the hours that the student spends looking at the books it would be more useful to set targets like are they able to argue both sides of a question. Are they able to apply the knowledge to a new situation; are they able to make fun of the knowledge and turn it into a joke? All of these things assist the storage and recall of the information and the ability to form views about what you are learning.

I had a good refresher course in these techniques a few years ago when I did a part-time course. After decades of skimming to see what I needed out of a book knowing that if I underlined it it would be easy for me to find, I suddenly found myself in a situation where I had to read a chapter and not know which bit I might be asked about. Once I had recovered from the full horror of knowing that I might need to know it all I reverted to my tried and trusted ways. I took an attitude to what the writer was saying. Everything was then measured against a criterion all the time and it either fitted into that world, or that world had to change.

I still find it hard not to get bored after an hour!

Anniversary 21 December 2003

Today would be my father's birthday. He would be 87 now. He died after a happy and largely healthy life three summers ago. We were not an especially close father and son. Golf was one of the few things we had in common. He worked in an insurance company which he enjoyed for about the first 25, grew to dislike after that and probably wholeheartedly loathed for the last five years as it became increasingly impersonal and target driven, a different business from the one he had joined as a teenager. He made sure that I had better opportunities. That pushed me away from his orbit at an early age, a distance that only closed to an adult-to-adult relationship in the last years of his life. As years go by the longing to have a loved one around still comes and goes.

The real physical pain that comes with grief shocks those of us who have lost a loved one. The stomach is hollow as never before, the chest tight until it hurts. People often find they are breathless and weak. Noise is so intrusive that it hurts. Then follows the gradual acceptance that the person is gone for good. Everyone's heart went out to Gerry Ryan on the radio talking about losing a filling. The first thought he had was that he would pop down to his dentist Dad to have it fixed, only to realise that he would never do that again. For a time people find it hard to function, but they soon accept the cold fact that the person will not return.

Vivid dreams of the person alive are common after sudden death. People are more prone to talk to the person as if they are there, sometimes sub-vocally. Some people become attached to a linking object associated with the dead person. This may be clothing, jewellery or letters. These linking objects are different from keepsakes in that the person becomes very anxious if they do not know where the object is. As they move through the grief process this practice, which can seem obsessional at times, gradually ceases to feel important.

Then there is the need to blame something or someone, and a sense of helplessness because of the assault on our neatly compartmentalised world. People question, even hate, the God who could have allowed this to happen, not unlike the reaction of a person on hearing their illness is terminal.

On a typical day, there is often one of your work colleagues who is dealing with the illness of a loved one or bereavement and they are doing their best to keep up with the job at the same time. They may not have even mentioned it at work. They are probably discovering that the only people who have much of an inkling about what is going on in their lives are the people who have already been there. Anyone who has been there knows that your brain and emotions go on automatic pilot. People are always surprised about how the experience affects them. It is usually not as they would have predicted. I still remember the phone call telling me my mother had a few weeks to live. I was calm. I took notes on what the doctor was telling me as if I was taking directions to an office. I put the phone down and, for the next 10 minutes, my voice refused to work. A colleague who stuck their head in the door assumed I had gone mad, or worse, and they retreated in embarrassment.

Grief hits people in different ways. Sometimes there are tears, sadness, and some anger. Or the person may become somewhat withdrawn from the hustle and bustle of life and a bit depressed. Often soon after the death people appear fine. A type of numbness sets in that protects the person from the full pain for a while. Most bereaved people feel a crushing fatigue for some time after the event and wonder will they ever shake the state of exhaustion they find themselves in. There are many sleepless nights in the time before and after a loss.

How work colleagues react can be a great help. If in a supervisory position, give the person some time off if the business can manage it. But the most important things you can do are listen and offer sympathy. People are often unsure about what to say. Well if that is the case just say you don't know what to say. But don't say you know how they feel unless you have been there. You don't.

Those who offer sympathy will feel helpless and useless. So too will the professional counsellors as they try to offer what assistance they can as each person muddles their way through the coming years. It is important to avoid platitudes such as pointing out that they are lucky to have lovely children and the like. About the only thing that can be truthfully said is 'you will get through it'.

The simple acknowledgement that you know what has happened matters. Nobody understands how important a handshake is at a funeral until they have received it. It matters and is felt. I still remember to my shame a group of teenage friends and myself who were too awkward to say anything when a friend outside our group lost his father. So, we went on as if nothing had happened. It was never mentioned. I suppose at some visceral level we felt that it could have been us and not him. If it came up, we would probably have pretended it was the first we had heard of it.

People adjust back at their own pace. But they often detest the things that are great fun normally. A loud party can be a nightmare. When my mother died I felt physical pain if there was some trashy soap on the television. For months, I could only tolerate two pieces of music – Mozart's *Requiem* and *Achtung Baby*.

The odd thing is that people usually function so well in this type of crisis that they assure all around them at work that they can cope fine. The reality is that they are completely over-stressed and it will be the best part of a year before they are back to normal. There are birthdays and special days to go through. One of the hurdles they have to get through is Christmas. For many people Christmas is the time of the year they dread, and once they are through it they are ready to face the world afresh, beginning to look forward again. They will appreciate some little understanding from you that while everyone is hyped up about presents, Santa, parties and all the rest that they are missing the person with whom they enjoyed those times in years past. No need to overdo it. But a few kind words won't go astray.

For the fully-healed person who thinks of the loved one who died there is always a sense of sadness, but there will come a day when there is the sadness, but without the pain. The mourning is complete. The person is able to love again.

9

Motivation and Getting Things Done

Praise – the oxygen of the office

Mol an óige agus tiocfaidh sí – Praise the young people and they will flourish. It is easy to catch them being bad and give out hell. The real trick is to catch them being good and let them know about it.

It doesn't take a great mind to realise that the consequences of what we do have a big impact on whether we do it again, and on how we feel about having done it in the first place. If a rat gets food for pressing a bar, it keeps on doing it. I am not too good on knowing a happy rat from an unhappy rat. But if a dog hears you saying 'good dog' his tail wags and you can see the smile on his face. We can all spot a happy dog. Just as we all know what a hangdog expression is!

Now we are a bit further up the food chain but, in some important regards, we are not very different from our less sophisticated distant relations. If children respond well to praise, it would be odd if there was a cut off point where adults didn't. Of course, they do. But we are more awkward about praising a grown up. The loss is ours. So, what are the ground rules for praising an adult?

I was on the receiving end of a bit of unexpected praise recently. The person in question concentrated on one or two things, and then as an afterthought asked me how I felt about what had been said. 'Well,' I stammered, 'it feels a bit odd to be getting praise at my stage in life!' With this episode fresh in my mind I went off to have a meal with a consistently successful woman, over 40, who had changed jobs recently. She was beaming as she had just opened a letter from some stratospherically placed senior executive complimenting her in detail on her performance. So, we ate contentedly like two 10-year-olds having got good marks in the *Feis Ceol*.

Praise, to be useful, has to be specific. So it isn't just *plamas*. We have all had the experience of the gushing person telling we are looking wonderful, etc., and we feel like a million dollars, only to hear the same speech half an hour later being delivered to someone who looks like they have been dragged through a bush backward! Deflated, or what?

You have to believe that the praiser knows what they are talking about. There was a time when the word 'excellent' was very much in vogue, and people were prattling on about things being 'excellent' when they hadn't a bull's notion of the standards required for good, bad, or indifferent. This is not praise. It is the person trying to pretend they know something that they don't.

So back to the rules. Being specific about what the praise is for is important. It is not that vague praise has no effect. It may even give a bit of a lift. But it does not provide much opportunity to learn.

In a work situation, some managers are uncomfortable with face-to-face praise and distance themselves by memos. These are good, but the traffic is one way. Face-to-face is better because it provides the opportunity for expansion and clarification. Having the meeting in private is usually most effective, and the person giving praise should strive to achieve empathy. It is important to be attuned to the impact of what you are saying if you are to engage at the appropriate level.

Effective managers lead by example so praise has an inherent worth if it comes from them. Effective managers are predictable in their response to how people perform, so it is clear to all that they are operating from well-founded standards, and it is not just the mood they are in.

Remember, you have to be around if you are to notice things worth noticing. So, get on with it. *Mol gach duine agus tiocfaidh siad.*

It's exam time - read the question

About 20 years ago I was editing a three-minute package for television and time was ticking away. We were up against it and I was new at the job. Looking back it was comical because the task was not huge. But with my level of competence, I was at the edge of my ability. Then as we neared the end, I heard my heart pounding like it had never pounded before. I sat there hoping nobody would notice. Hoping it would go away. I got up and walked out of the room, sure that something was badly wrong. Was this the first stage of a heart attack, I wondered? Had moving to television been a disastrous mistake?

The work was finished on time and I was a shadow of my former self. I had not been sick ever apart from normal childhood illnesses. Now I wondered was I going to be struck down prematurely for all the boasting I did about being healthy. I didn't even have a GP, so I went to see a GP friend in a new capacity – patient to doctor.

I told him the story. He told me it was a perfectly normal response to stress. Nothing to worry about. 'And that,' he said, 'is the standard spiel that I have been giving since I started in medicine. I thought that was fine until the same thing happened to me six months ago and it scared the living daylights out of me and I wasn't happy until I had had every test under the sun!'

We laughed it off. I learned how to do the job. It went from being stressful to a doddle. But I tell the story because so many of us are in a position of dispensing advice to people on a regular basis, and it is difficult to remember that we may not have the remotest idea of what they are experiencing. Which brings me to my exams.

I regularly talk to people who are a bit stressed out. Maybe they are facing some test or other at work. Or some new challenge that will take place in front of people and they are nervous about it. They do not like being watched. They may worry that they will be talked about, or even laughed about. Their big concern is that these worries will stop them doing as well as they are capable of. They might even fail.

I always thought I did a good job getting them in the right frame of mind. Now I wonder. For I have led a pretty stress-free life in those areas. Fear of failure did not haunt me. Until now. I have not done enough reading and my exam is a few short weeks away. Just how did I get into this mess and what will I do about it.

Any area of work is constantly changing and it is becoming the norm to continue education through one's career. There are new ideas to explore, new people to meet, and old cobwebs to sweep away. So, with that in mind two years ago I decided to do a part-time course in psychotherapy. I figured it would be no problem. Then the workload began to pile up and gradually I realised I was falling behind. Not only that but the exams were getting nearer and nearer. Now I have not failed an exam since fifth grade piano (I didn't practise) and suddenly I realised I was in the danger zone. I began to imagine just how I would feel. Instead of working, I began to hear 'the voices'. My eyes are on the page. My mind is rehearsing telling people how I should never have embarked on the course because I just don't have time. There is probably a part of my unconscious considering getting sick on exam day!

So, I have no choice. I talk to myself as if I were someone else. I prioritise the work. I do my self-hypnosis, step into the difficult situation, and see myself doing well. I call up from my memory past times when I was under pressure and relive the feelings of coping and succeeding. Just as if I was another person.

The anxiety is under control. I will do what is required. It is not as if it is going to be on the nine o'clock news!

Maybe the next time I am asked to give someone a bit of help I will have a better idea of what I am talking about. How about you?

Absenteeism - they've got the flu again!

How often have you looked around the office and seen the person next to you is not in? Yet again. Every time it happens you pick up the slack. You start to wonder are you a total fool and are determined that this time they can do their own catching up.

Or you are a middle manager in a large organisation and your daily headache is figuring out how to keep the show on the road with a few people off each day. Monday's are the worst. Let's be honest. Have you ever taken a day off with an invented cold when in reality you were just a bit fed up with the job? Or maybe a bit hungover? What one person gets a day out of, another thinks is good for three days, while some take the full week. Then there is the related problem of people who are physically in the building but for all the work they do, they may as well be elsewhere.

You have probably heard the martyrs in the office and at home telling you that they don't get sick because they cannot get sick. It is all very well for you who can take to the bed at the slightest hint of a sniffle but they will carry on. If you stop to think you will soon come up with a list of people at work who succumb to several colds each winter and take their full allocation of sick days, some people who soldier through it (and probably infect everyone in the vicinity) and then there are those who seem almost immune to the common cold. Why is this?

The bigger the organisation the more absenteeism is a headache. In a small company, everyone is vital and knows they are and people will keep working until they can hardly stand. In fact, they will have to be told to go home for their own sake. The self-employed just do not have any choice. If they do not work, they are not paid. Insurance to cover time off work due to illness is so expensive that many people do not have any cover.

The stories of the worker who calls in from their sickbed only to be caught on camera putting €10 on the 3.30 pm at Leopardstown are well known. So, what can be done about it?

Well it is becoming clear that there are many psychological and lifestyle factors that influence whether or not you will get a cold. Much of the research has been done by measuring emotions and life events in volunteers and then giving them a dose of rhinovirus which causes colds. This is sprayed into the subject's nose and they are then monitored over the next week or so to see how they fare. Sure enough, your attitude to life has a big impact on whether you get sick or not!

One important measure is positive emotional style. People who are vigorous, have a good sense of well-being and feel calm about life score high on this. People who are depressed, anxious or hostile score low. It turns out that people who score low are three times more likely to get sick than those high on positive style. The people with negative emotional styles reported more symptoms than would be expected by the clinical signs they showed. In short, they were more likely to get sick and when they did, they made more of it.

How many friends and acquaintances you have is also relevant. The more diverse your network of people is the less likely you are to get a cold. Being socially isolated is not good for your health and other studies have found that people with a rich array of relationships in their life also have a better chance of surviving after a heart attack and less likelihood of suffering a recurrence of cancer. It seems that there is something about occupying a variety of roles in life … spouse, parent, colleague, friend, customer in the local shop, charity organiser, etc … that promotes resistance to infection. It may be that having that range of roles helps us feel good about ourselves and keeps us more positive. This gets further complicated because people with few friends are also more likely to smoke and less likely to exercise and these are not helpful habits.

Some companies try to reward attendance and this has the obvious benefits that everyone knows what the rules are and know what they have to do. One large Irish company cut their absenteeism by 50% by instituting a good reward programme. As well as going some way towards solving the problem, this is proof, if proof were needed, that much of the sickness was not sickness at all.

Another approach is to look in a practical way at factors that may help a worker decide to take the day off. This can include things as varied as transport problems, dealing with sick children, or helping people recognise and deal with excessive drinking.

The organisational culture is tackled by many companies to try to create a climate where people feel their input is valued and that the company takes absence seriously. Job involvement has a big impact on a person's commitment to their work, as does the perception that they are being paid fairly. If people feel underpaid, they feel that bit more entitled to take some time off.

One of the most important influences on how often workers will get sick is the presence of paid leave for a number of days for people calling in sick. The evidence is clear. If the days are there, many people will take them whether sick or not. Sick days soon become viewed by many as just another form of holidays. It doesn't cost people anything to stay at home, so why not?

Stress is well know to have an effect on the immune system and not surprisingly studies show that people who have experienced negative things in their life over the past year, for example bereavement, loss of job, or just plain back luck, are more likely to succumb to infection. So, what can one do to reduce one's susceptibility apart from take a more positive approach to life?

Well, the good news is that moderate consumption of alcohol reduces your chances of getting a cold. As does moderate levels of exercise. So apparently does eating a good breakfast. Echinacea taken for eight weeks reduces your likelihood of getting a cold by a third. If you do get one then taking doses of vitamin C usually shortens the duration of the illness by a day or two. While you are suffering, your ability to perform many routine tasks is not as good as usual. More good news is that this is an excuse to up your caffeine intake, as coffee is a great help in keeping you functioning at a satisfactory level if you are below par.

If you are determined to escape the dreaded virus then probably the best way to stay clear is to work on your mood. We have a lot more control over our mood than we admit. To a degree, you can make a choice as to whether you want to feel down in the dumps or take a more optimistic outlook. If you find that your social life has become a bit narrow and predictable it is not too late to get out and meet some new people, and keep in contact with the ones you know. It makes life more pleasant. The bonus is that it is good for your health.

A lot of this points to the value of small teams of people working together in a situation where they can get to know each other personally and understand each other's importance on a daily basis, working together for everyone's benefit. That probably more than anything explains the difference between the person who drags themselves out of bed come hail, rain or snow, and the person who regards every tiny sniffle as the mother and father of a dose of flu.

Which reminds me, when did everyone stop talking about the common cold and just refer to everything as 'the flu'? Anyone who has ever had the flu will tell you that it is a very different beast indeed.

Ambition – or why Paul McCartney still wants a No. 1

I have come across many ambitious people in my time and they all have one thing in common. They seem to get somewhere. Usually when they get somewhere, they are motivated to stay there, or get even further. People may mellow with age but I am sure Paul McCartney would dearly love to top the charts one more time. Margaret Thatcher probably still wants to be prime minister and Sonia O'Sullivan is still thinking about the gold medals she can win.

People who get places are often described as having great drive – a quality psychologists say is made up of a need for achievement, ambition and high energy levels. They are quite simply not like other people. They know where they want to be and they are going there.

Is this always admirable? Not necessarily so. We all know the phrase 'blind ambition' and many of us have seen it at work. In the media everyone has come across people who would walk over their granny to get on television or have their picture in the paper. As an end in itself it does seem shallow. The lust for their 15 minutes of fame is strong.

In business, anyone will be able to think of somebody whose only ambition was to get to the top. If that involves relentless effort, currying favour, social networking, often deceit, bullying and sacrificing many things that more rounded people would value, then so be it. Sometimes such people also possess the important skills necessary for good leadership and decision-making, sometimes they do not and they turn out to be disastrous managers. Recruitment agencies do their clients a good favour if they can weed out these people.

But a more balanced form of ambition is essential to the development of both our community and our personal lives. A need for achievement is made up of a number of qualities or personality traits – the desire to work hard, the pursuit of excellence, the aspiration to climb up a hierarchy, the enjoyment of competition, pursuit of money, and, very importantly, the satisfaction obtained from successfully completing projects and solving problems.

The Irish work ethic has come under some scrutiny by researchers over the years and it never comes out with flying colours. Makes you wonder how the Celtic Tiger every happened! We are always found to have lower achievement needs than our American counterparts. Though oddly once the Irish leave Ireland we tend to work as hard, or harder than anybody.

Economists sometimes complain that one of the curses of the Irish economy is that an entrepreneur will build up a small to medium company and then have no interest in developing it further. The reasons are simple. The person is making enough money and more doesn't make sense if it is at the expense of family, leisure, games of golf and their health. Now that sounds eminently sensible to me.

It is an unusual person who remains single-mindedly dedicated from beginning to end on one goal. The gifted achiever branches out. Like Bono and the focus on world debt. A man who has done plenty says he want to start doing things – things that make a difference. Probably things that were implanted in his personality as a child and never went away.

Recent American research shows that today's teenagers are the most ambitious generation ever. I expect Irish children who have grown up in a changed and thriving Ireland are no different. But the downside is that these teenagers are much less directed by their schools and parents than they need to be, with the result that many feel alienated, friendless and even depressed. Without guidance and skills, their dreams will remain just that, dreams.

I recently asked a woman who had a string of accomplishments to her name if she thought of herself as ambitious. She thought for a while, and decided that she didn't think she was ambitious for herself, but she was for her children.

What did she mean by that. Again some thought.

'Well I would like them to lead happy, healthy, fulfilling and productive lives. I suppose the things I do with them and for them are to help in those directions in so far as I can'.

Now that seemed to me like a worthwhile ambition.

Brainstorming – the simple joy of knocking heads together

Two heads are better than one. Well not always. If there are more than two people, do things get better or worse? We have all heard the one-liners about committees. A committee is a cul de sac down which ideas are lured and then quietly strangled. Or one wit said that a committee should consist of three people, two of whom are absent.

Well committees are one thing but part of a lot of people's working week is a brainstorming session. Whatever occupation you are in, ideas are probably the lifeblood of the enterprise and typically great importance is attached to the brainstorming session to come up with some new ones. But does it work? What goes on? Can it be made more effective? We have all sat with groups, week in, week out and seen the same people shine while others try to hide. But perhaps they have just as many ideas, or fewer and better ones, but the format does not suit them.

The rules of brainstorming are simple – all ideas are welcome, however bizarre they might seem at first because you never know what they might spark off. The more ideas the better, and people should not criticise them, because there just might be something in there that will lead somewhere. The ideas belong to the group, not to the individual. Many people have difficulty with this as in a public group it takes self-confidence to share ideas. You have to feel there are loads more where that one came from.

In theory, it all sounds fine. But in practice? First, groups have freeloaders. As others throw things in, they do less. They often make as much noise, but if you look carefully, freeloaders are just restating what has been said and not much more. There are those who constantly censor themselves for fear of feeling foolish or of being ridiculed. Finally, in groups everyone's work output tends to drop towards that of the lower performers.

To a degree, a good leader can deal with these problems. But it is an uphill battle, and requires a degree of social and intellectual skills not present in many managers. If the leader is to keep the quality up, they have to be well capable of setting the standard high and being seen to be well up to it.

Brainstorming has not turned out to be all it was cracked up to be, but some organisations are addicted to it. Most probably, there is a social function to it. It is an opportunity for a few jokes, to get to know people better, and it creates the illusion that a lot was accomplished. For these reasons alone perhaps it should happen now and again, but it you want better work rates and ideas there are better ways.

Electronic brainstorming is coming increasingly into vogue. I am not one of those who think computers are the answer to everything. I am the first to acknowledge the tyranny of the e-mail, the bullying possibilities of its thoughtless use, and the plain rudeness that it can foster. In developing ideas, it is turning out to be far better than the face to face.

For donkey's years studies have shown that people are more productive working alone, and computers let us work alone, together. You can jot down your idea whenever you like and circulate it when you feel it is worth looking at. You don't have to wait your turn and sit back while some other half-baked notion is distracting you. From a manager's point of view, you can see just who is coming up with the goods and what their strengths are, and because people are not paying as much attention to the performance of others, they tend to work to their own beat, and that is more productive.

So maybe two heads aren't that much better than one. But two terminals are. The best committee may be when everyone is absent – but able to log on when they have something worthwhile to say.

Next time there are eight of you around a table pause for thought and ask just what do you think you are all doing.

Procrastination - or one more cup of coffee

You often hear it said that if you want a job done ask a busy person to do it. There is definitely a lot of truth in it. People who do a lot find it easy to do a little more. They are good at looking at what has to be done and setting about it, and usually not giving themselves a pat on the back until they have more or less cleared the decks, certainly cleared the decks of what can be done in that particular day.

At the opposite end of the continuum are those who just cannot get started and when they do get started leave things unfinished. These are the 'procrastination is the thief of time' people, but no one has to steal the time from them. They are giving it away with both hands.

We all go through periods of not being able to get going and putting things off. Temptation looms everywhere. Most writers facing the blank page will tell you that there are days when cleaning the bathroom seems like the most attractive thing on the planet. Or at a lesser level you have that one more cup of coffee before you start, or read the paper from cover to cover, including the racing results even if you don't know one end of a horse from the other! If there is a task to be done and you feel an irresistible desire to tidy everything then you are showing one of the vital signs of a procrastinator.

The first big mistake a procrastinator makes is putting the reward before the work, and the secret weapon the busy person has is the ability to delay reward for long periods. They wait until a substantial amount has been accomplished. Most busy people also make sure they build in some mega rewards, and so they feel entitled to that week in the sun, or whatever, and they enjoy it to the full.

Oddly, procrastination is one of the few negative characteristics that people freely admit to. Maybe this is because they see it as part of what they are and believe there is nothing they can do about it. But that is rubbish. We can easily take control of our thoughts and behaviour and get on with it. This time-wasting is a sizeable problem. Studies find that about one in five adults identifies themselves as chronic procrastinators. It has become a lifestyle for them.

The results are significant. It had been repeatedly demonstrated that students who leave things to the last minute do not do as well in their university assessments. If this behaviour is carried through to adulthood and the work environment where deadlines are more flexible then the person is setting himself or herself up to feel inadequate, guilty and plagued by self-doubt.

How did they get like that? In many cases, it may be a response to an authoritarian parenting style which does not allow children to develop the ability to regulate their own behaviour. But the causes are probably more complex than that. If you have this problem do you recognise any of the following in your work style? Are you a perfectionist who just cannot do things that will live up to your expectations? Are you the sort of person who is over concerned about what others will think of you? Do you see tasks as overwhelming? Or are you one of those people who tells yourself and others that you work best under pressure? You may think you do, but you don't, and you cause havoc all around when you are screaming at the photocopier to hurry up or tearing your hair out when the computer crashes. Finally are you one of those people who can only work when 'in the right mood'? Well, the best way to get in the right mood is to get started. Your mood won't change by itself.

A good trick many people use is the 30-minute plan. Do a half-hour of work and give yourself a reward at the end. It may be a phone call, a television programme, a walk in the garden. Whatever.

But do the half-hour and surprise, surprise, you many find yourself putting off the reward instead of putting off the work.

I've got a little list

'I've got a little list'. I think that particular refrain came from the Lord High Executioner in the *Mikado* and it was no doubt of great assistance to him in his line of work!

I confess that I am a bit of a martyr to lists. I am truly happy when I sit down with someone, each of us armed with our checklists, and stay at it until we have worked our way through. The reason I am happy is that I am convinced that this is the best way to minimise the drudge aspects of work and get on with doing something else.

Lists have their good points. If it is written down, there is a good chance it will be done. Sadly, I have to write it down, otherwise, I will completely forget about it. It would be no harm to get back a bit of creativity. I admire those people who can go into the supermarket, shop for six meals simultaneously and change the menus mid stream. I come out with what is on the list. What starts out as an aid to memory can mean that memory almost closes down!

Back to the positive. *Tús maith, leath na hoibre*. Some task lists have an important role in preparing the mind for what is ahead. One that is very useful is the list you write in the last ten minutes in the office. I once worked with a woman who had this routine down to a fine art. As she went about things through the day her A4 page would get more and more messy with things crossed out, notes added, arrows from here to there, phone numbers, names, dates and places everywhere. Then as the day drew to a close she would take out a new page and neatly order what needed to be done the next day, place it in the middle of her desk and leave without a care in the world.

So, what is going on for the person using this system? Well, first they finish the day with a good reminder of what they have accomplished during the day. Even on the worst days, there will always have been things that will give some satisfaction.

Secondly, it is a great way to mark the difference between work and the rest of your life. Tomorrow is set out as just that, tomorrow, and there is no point in bothering to worry about it until then. The person who leaves their work at work can go out and enjoy themselves without work problems niggling at them. The mind is an odd thing. You will find that the only time work does pop into your consciousness is with something positive, like a solution. The unconscious has been working away in the background with tomorrow's list while you are completely untroubled by it.

Finally, when tomorrow does arrive you hit the ground running. When you know where to start, it is easy to get going.

This type of system tends to appeal to people who enjoy their work, but want to keep it from taking over the rest of their lives. Lee Iaccoco who achieved fame as a super-executive in the American motor industry had a similar approach. He liked to keep his weekends sacred from work, and did so from Friday to Sunday evening. Then each Sunday evening he took an hour alone in his study to familiarise himself with the week ahead. Then back to home life, the rest of the weekend, and he already had a jump on Monday.

One final thing. What do you do with that item that stays on the list and just will not go away? You have to do something with it or else it becomes like that bathroom wall with 'tiles here' written on it for so long that people don't see it. If something isn't going off the list then take some time to examine why. Then either find a way to do it, or forget about it – don't have it looking at you morning after morning making you feel guilty.

So, that is this written. Time to cross it off and have a cup of coffee.

Set your goals ... some talk ... some do it

There are those who talk about it and those who do it. I can think of people who manage to transform their house between visits. The garden will have been tackled. Something major will have been painted. Or there will be a conservatory where once there was an ugly yard but potential suntrap. These people see the potential and do something about it.

Then there are those who come back after the summer holidays all full of resolutions to watch less television and by Christmas they are proudly showing you their new DVD and wide screen television. To remind them of their August intentions would seem churlish as they explain to you what a good deal it was. We all know eternal students who are writing that thesis for as long as we can remember!

It is partly 'those who can, do', but crucially 'those who plan, do'. An oft-quoted study began in Yale University in 1953 when students were asked if they had written down their goals and a plan for achieving them. Only 3% had done so. Twenty years later, it turned out that the 3% with specific goals were worth more than the remaining 97%. Now money isn't everything, and I always feel this research lost nothing in the telling, but clearly, something is going on here. It is comforting that the 3% also scored well on other life measures such as happiness.

Some people seem to just let life happen to them. Their job doesn't satisfy them but they don't do anything about it. Every year they plan a night course, and every year it passes and all they feel is resentment as others who were on a par with them move on and on and on.

The key to getting from A to B is to know where B is. If you don't know what you want, you won't get it – you are the only person who can get you there. So, think it out. Set the goal and write it down. The self-help books all tell us that once you really decide to do something you can do almost anything you want. Take it with a slight pinch of salt, but there is a scary amount of truth in it. Ask any ex-cigarette smoker what was different about the time they quit and all the other previous attempts. Usually it is a variation of 'this time I decided to do it'.

So, make a list. Sort it out whatever way you like ... short-term and long-term ... life-changing or just something small ... work or leisure ... relationships, at work and at home. Some you will really want to do. Some you might just feel like. Suit yourself but take two quiet hours and get it written.

You will probably find that what you have written falls into five categories. They will be to do with knowing things (finally learning German), doing things (the marathon, joining a bridge club, growing cabbages, visiting Cuba), getting things (from a leather jacket to a house), relating with people (your boss, your Aunt Jane, your partner, children, or the neighbours) and finally being (be it slimmer, fitter, richer, funnier, etc.). Have a good look and put them in the order that is important to you. In an afternoon, you will have learned a lot about yourself – and don't lie!

So how to get where you want to get – a few simple ideas will help. Check if the goals are reasonably specific. Is there a clear difference between getting there and not getting there? Ask yourself why? Do you want to lose that seven pounds because you need to or somebody else tells you that you need to? Do you want that diploma because it is relevant to your career or just to generally boost your self-esteem?

Are the things on your list things that you can exercise a lot of influence over by your own behaviour? If success or failure depend on you, excuses are much harder to come by. Ask yourself realistically – is what you have written down within your reach. You probably won't become a scratch golfer.

Next, think of what other things will be affected if you get what you want. Changing your job or achieving more responsibility in your work will affect the relationships with your partner, children, friends and workmates. Some will be good and some will be not so good. Think through the likely scenarios, make up your mind, write it down and go for it.

New year resolutions

It happens every December. No matter how your year went, there are things about yourself that you would like to be different in the coming year. You probably had a conversation with yourself about a year ago and were full of resolve, most of which had fallen by the wayside by early January. If it were as easy as saying 'I'll cut down on the drink', and doing it, the publicans would be a dying breed. But the publicans know better than the rest of us that good intentions are usually followed by a return to old habits and they see their businesses surviving all the nonsense that people promise themselves in the final few days of the year.

One recent study found that people are about five times more likely to decide to increase behaviour than to stop doing something. About two-thirds of the people surveyed made three or more resolutions. The most common goal was increasing the amount of exercise taken, being chosen by more than a third of people. Next was to increase the time spent on study or at work which was chosen by a quarter. Thirteen percent wanted to increase the amount of good food eaten and decrease the junk and 7% wanted to cut down on alcohol or caffeine. The surprising thing about this research was that after two months two-thirds of the people were sticking to their resolution. One suspects that this was partly because people were aware they were part of a study and that helped them to keep focusing on what they wanted to change. But that in itself gives us a good clue as to an important factor in bringing about lasting change: *monitor your behaviour*.

The other heartening thing researchers found was that persistence pays off. Most people who achieved their resolution did not do so at their first attempt. No, they tried, and failed, and then tried again. About one in five people who were successful were on their sixth attempt. So, do not be too hard on yourself if you have a setback. Just start all over again and it might be a bit easier this time.

People decide what they are going to change in the last few

days of the year and these are days when you have been out of your normal routine and over-indulging for days, or weeks. A lot of people are looking forward to getting some structure back into their lives, 'back to brass tacks' my mother used to say, so it is easy to be full of good intentions. Unless you do some planning, your intentions will crumble once you are back in that routine that seemed so attractive when bloated and lazy. This is because to feel the effects of behaviour change takes time. It would be fine if you could go for your walk, come back, and find that four ounces had been shed on the pavement and that you were guaranteed nearly two pounds the first week. Sadly, it doesn't work like that. You may even put on weight as you replace fat with muscle. So, you have to take a long-term view and then one day you do notice your belt feeling that bit looser. Once you reach that stage it is easier to continue.

The second killer to resolutions is that changing your behaviour doesn't make you immediately happier. It may indeed do the opposite. So again, you have to go through the bad times to get to the good. Keeping a note each day of how you are doing will help. The three strongest predictors of success are *keeping track of your progress, having a strong initial commitment to change*, and *having some plans in mind for dealing with problems that will come up*. If you are going to a wedding in a few weeks' time be realistic about what you will do that day.

If you decide what you want to change impulsively on New Year's Eve, your chances are about nil. As they are if you vow you are absolutely deciding never to do whatever it is ever again. The bar is too high. Or more importantly, the bar is still serving drink!

Get psyched up for change. Close you eyes and take some time to visualise what it will be like if you succeed. List all the benefits. Set realistic dates to get there. Keep checking how you are doing. You mightn't be where you want to be. But it is good to know you are on the way.

Get focused

Concentration is a funny thing. There are days when your mind wanders all over the place and nothing seems to focus your thoughts. You know the feeling of reaching the bottom of a page having gone through the motions of reading but without a single word being remembered. You go back to the top again and it doesn't seem even vaguely familiar.

Concentration is a focusing of our attention on the matter in hand. Attention is much harder to control than the physical side of our being. When walking along the street it will take a good push from somebody to put us off our course. But we can be deep in thought and have it shattered immediately by a noise, an unexpected visual stimulus, or hearing our name even if it is not intended for us but for someone of the same name. Everyone knows the 'cocktail party' phenomenon when amidst all the buzz you are distracted by hearing something of interest to you, your name, the town you live in, the score of a football match, and immediately your mind flicks to the far side of the room. You realise the difficulty of your mind attending to two things at once when you switch back to the people you were talking with and face the embarrassing situation of not having a clue what has just been said.

A lot of the study of the importance of concentration and focus when carrying out physical and mental tasks has been with sports people. Any athlete will tell you that they can train to the peak of condition and then have their mind let them down, so they see great importance in having the mind in the right place when they are competing. Golfers will remember the great Jack Nicklaus playing one of the worst rounds of his career in the British Open years ago. He was in perfect condition, playing well the day before and yet he scored in the eighties, unheard of for the Golden Bear. The reason? His son had been injured in a car crash and Jack, like any father, was worried and couldn't keep his mind on the job. This from the man who was one of the first to speak about the steps he went through to get the mind and body working together. His routine when he prepared to hit a golf shot was so methodical that he said his mind refused to allow him to hit the ball until every muscle was in the correct place. Then, wham, it happened.

Jack hit on one of the important aids to concentration. Routine. Many people who need to concentrate during the day, writers for instance, have a routine that they use to settle down and frequently a place that is set aside for work. Once in the situation, they get into a zone where the mind attends to the work and it is done. In this place, they keep distractions to a minimum. Setting aside a time when you will not be disturbed is a good way of getting some work done. Using a kitchen timer can free the mind to attend to the task for whatever duration you like. First set it for 10 minutes and you will find you are so absorbed when it beeps that it gives you quite a start. Build up the time until you find it easy to do an hour of uninterrupted and focused work. It gets easy to put all the other cares of life out of your mind because you know you have 23 other hours to do them. The same system works well for students trying to get into a good study habit. Start practising now and it will be a piece of cake in the run up to summer exams.

Keeping distractions at bay is important for concentration. But what is a distraction one day is barely noticed another day. The tennis player who is in the groove never notices the photographers in the crowd. But when body and mind are not in harmony, every movement catches their eye. GAA players will tell you about injuries that are not noticed when you are ahead, but feel painful when losing.

Concentration is a bit like a mental muscle. Find a place, develop a routine and minimise the outside distractions and slowly the most difficult distractions of all, the ones in your own head, are assigned to a different time and place.

PPPPPP

I have a friend who has a reminder in big capital letters on the notice board in his office. It reads P P P P P P. Not surprisingly, people often ask him what it is about and he relishes the moment. It stands for *Plenty of Practice Prevents a P....ing Poor Performance*.

I often think of the Gary Player story when he holed a chip for 30 yards off the green only to hear someone in the gallery remark that it was a very lucky shot. 'Yes,' he said, 'and the more I practise the luckier I get'.

Behaviour of all sorts tends to be stuck in a groove. If something works, we keep on doing it the same way. But lots of the time what works is not the best way to do something. There is not a lot of difference between a groove and a rut. You have to learn a new way of doing it to get a better result. This is where the practice comes in. I was very conscious of this as a motorbike trainer put me through my paces recently. As he talked to me through an earpiece, he made me do things repeatedly until they became second nature. I went around a roundabout more time than most humans do in a month, but guess what, now I do it right and it feels natural.

But my friend of the six Ps was neither a sportsman nor a driving instructor. He is a social skills trainer who helps people who have difficulties in relating to people to become better at it. They may have a problem saying what they mean, making phone calls, asking for directions, etc. I remember him telling me of one person who had to practise meeting people at parties and getting a conversation going. They would role-play in the office, practise at home and then that person had to go out and do the real thing and report on their progress. It may have been a bit stilted at first. Then they were able to do five minutes. But they practised until it became second nature. Eventually they made a friend which is what it was all about.

Too often, when we prepare for something we prepare in our heads. We imagine the first few words of the conversation and probably put in the other person's replies. But preparing in your head while helping you focus, is a bit like preparing for your French oral exam without opening your mouth. It is fine to imagine yourself singing like Freddie Mercury but the muscles and vocal chords need to be exercised too if you are to improve. I notice that many foreign workers in shops in Ireland now repeat back to you what you ask for. This is partially for clarity but I am sure they are also consciously practising to improve what they sound like in English. All that on top of a day's work but in my local the progress is huge. Some of them are now throwing in a few words *as Gaeilge*.

There are many conversations and social situations we encounter at work that we might wish to change. There may be things about how the job is carried out that you would like to discuss with colleagues or a line manager. How that conversation begins is a good omen for how it will progress, so practice may make it feel easier.

The job interview is a classic. To go into a job interview without having been grilled in rehearsal by friends or colleagues is deliberately handicapping yourself. Older readers will remember the famous six hours of television interview between David Frost and Richard Nixon. Legend has it that Nixon's preparation with his team was so thorough that there was only one question that he had not rehearsed the answer to.

Nowadays many jobs are a succession of interviews. From the plumber quoting for a job to the public relations team pitching for a project, people are performing to get work. Talent and experience alone do not gain the work. It depends, in part, on how one performs at the pitch. When there is a lot at stake it is worth setting aside the time to train, rehearse and practise.

Remember, whether it is your golf swing or how you sell an idea, PPPPPP.

I've got an agenda

I had a bit of a break recently and there is nothing like clear blue skies and drinking bubbly at Irish bottled water prices to get you thinking 'I could do with a little more of this'. Your mind drifts back to the many things you do that waste time. Top of my list is that vision of 10 people sitting around a table discussing something or other without much enthusiasm and then heading off scratching their heads wondering what all that was about. Yes, we have all been at unproductive meetings – finalising a budget or deciding who does what at the car boot sale. They eviscerate enthusiasm, eke away your energy and puncture your passion.

Now I have always been a fan of lists. Last thing at night, first thing in the morning and repeatedly through the day I am putting lines though one list and writing another. It isn't done if it isn't crossed off the list and it won't be done if it doesn't get on the list. Even with a throbbing toothache, I am probably likely to write down 'dentist' before making the phone call.

A proper meeting comes with its own built-in list – called an 'agenda'. Any time you are at a meeting where there isn't an agenda, head for the window and prepare to jump. When a meeting is called, make sure you know who is putting together the agenda. Then at least you can start with a piece of paper with some things to cross out on it!

An agenda is a powerful document because it lists the order in which things will be discussed and it often takes a lot to shift that order. Things can of course are added on, but often they are lumped in under 'other business' and do not get the treatment they deserve. So it is important for people to communicate before the meeting the items they will bring to the meeting that need some discussion with the people who are present. Otherwise, don't whinge if your topic gets the 30-second treatment or worse, 'we'll discuss that next week'.

Meetings tell a lot about the culture of the organisation you work in. Ideally, you should come out fired up about the progress made on various fronts and excited about the feedback you have on your own projects and ready to move things on with the support of enthusiastic colleagues. But how often have you been part of a group who leave the room muttering 'now let's get back to doing some real work'?

Yet, increasingly in today's complex world the meeting *is* the 'real work'. It is from the meeting that the energy of the company flows and if it isn't flowing then the company is asleep on its feet. So organisations are looking at ways to make the time decision-makers spend together more productive. Think of the times you have spoken to your line manager asking for a decision and are told it will be trashed out at Tuesday's meeting. You are all ready to go only to be told on Tuesday afternoon that no decision was taken and they will get back to it next week. It is frustrating, demoralising and who could blame any employee from throwing their hands in the air.

We go to a meeting, which is a noun, but we do not go there to meet people, a verb. We go there to get things done. It would focus the mind more to think of going to a 'doing' than a 'meeting'. A meeting is what happens when you bump into an old friend on Grafton Street and retire to Bewleys for a chat.

Where do your meetings take place? Often they are in sterile rooms with none of the equipment available to present data relevant to decisions. Do you need a flip chart? Or a photocopier? How many people will bring laptops? First and foremost, have an environment suitable to focusing the people on the issues, and the equipment to ensure that all can have the relevant information readily available. If the information isn't there, the decision is postponed. If you want to know how much that costs just look at the number of people in the room and do the multiplication of their hourly rate and then add a big chunk for the disruption spread among those who work in their departments!

Create an environment where people can take the meeting seriously. Otherwise, they will arrive late and spend their time doodling. When things are moving the meeting-room should resemble the Ferrari pit stop a great deal more than the work canteen.

I am back at work – and with an agenda.

Hot groups

Every now and again, you come across a group of people so fired up about a task they are determined to achieve that you get the feeling that nothing on earth will stop them. I remember one such group on the political campaign trail when Bill Clinton was the not very well known governor of Arkansas. But the lights were on in the eyes of the people working for him. Late nights were no problem to these people. Going the extra mile didn't raise an eyebrow. Doing the impossible was all in a day's work.

When you think of behaviour like this examples spring to mind from voluntary work and charity projects more easily than in the office. But they do happen in the world of work too and the nucleus that created the Apple computer is often cited as an example of a collection of people on a mission. In the workplace, intensely focused enthusiastic groups have been referred to as 'hot groups'. An American researcher who coined the term says that these people give new meaning to the notion of 'loving your job'. How to create such a group is a challenge for every manager with an important goal in mind.

There is a massive difference between people who are driven to complete a project with a group of colleagues and workaholics. If you look around your workplace, you will immediately spot the difference. People in a hot group would probably love to be in the swimming pool but just for now there is something more important to do. When they accomplish what they set out to do, they will happily revert to normal leisure activities until the next big challenge takes over.

People need to be really turned on by the task to get absolutely absorbed by it. A few things help. Intense competition is important when people come together to pitch for a project and must complete their proposal by a particular deadline. They know who the competition are and they are determined to knock their socks off.

A crisis can also help. Last year I watched a group of actors and film crew work for 24 solid hours to turn a field into something resembling the botanic gardens. Why did they do it? The quickest, most economical, way to get the location needed was to make it – and they would have walked on hot coals for the boss, Brendan O'Carroll.

Another great motivator that can excite passion is a worthwhile idea. Bob Geldof motivated the world with Live Aid. Bono is changing thinking with the Drop the Debt campaign.

Meaning is important to people and whether it is making a film or advancing a humanitarian cause it is important that the activity makes people feel real and vital. They feel their soul is being fed as well as other needs. They are turned on by the knowledge that what they are doing really matters and will make a difference. That is why you often find groups like this in universities who are researching a problem that is fully engaging, making progress all the time, feeling the breakthrough is around the corner, and knowing it will change people's lives in the fullness of time.

Leadership is vital for the maintenance of passion and intensity. The best leaders are those who manage to combine strong individuality with the ability to be team players. They can go out in front, do solo runs, and are often multi-talented. But they are also able to roll up their sleeves and get their hands dirty. Bill Clinton would have stuffed envelopes if that was what needed to be done in between giving interviews with well-aimed sound bites. Crucial for this type of leadership is that they always *share* the glory.

One final thing about hot groups. They are light on bureaucracy. They do not tend to see bureaucracy as the glue that holds them together, but more as the sludge that slows them down. Hot groups are often time-based because you cannot stay passionate forever whether in love or in work. But like love the more flexible and adaptable the structure the longer the flames of passion will burn.

Learning

Right up to the day we die humans are learning. There are always things to do that we have never done before and frequently through life, we make a decision to learn something new, only to give up before it is accomplished. To learn something new requires patience, determination and effort and we may just feel it is all too much hassle and give up.

I am always struck by the hours put in by sports people to get a particular technique and movement just right until it feels like the most natural thing in the world. I see it with singers and actors on the stage who rehearse and rehearse until their performance appears to be just effortless. These people know about the stages of learning and they know that they have to keep at it until it feels as natural to them as walking down the street. They know there are no short cuts.

Knowledge of the stages that one goes through in learning a new skill may just help people persevere through the difficult stages. For anyone who has recently learned to drive a car, taken golf lessons, taken up a musical instrument, or learned to swim these stages will feel very familiar indeed.

The first stage could be called blissful ignorance. You are not able to do something and you are not even aware that you are unable to do it. It could be that it has just never occurred to you to paint a picture or make a bookshelf or whatever.

Then for some reason or other you decide that you would like to learn something new. You watch people who are able to do it with ease and are fully aware that your muscles just will not do what you want them to do. Have you ever tried skiing? Anyone who has can remember the early helpless days of having no control with the instructor telling you to do x, y, and z and feeling like an absolute moron because you cannot do the simplest thing right – while five year olds are whizzing past you like experts. At this stage you are conscious of what you want to do and fully conscious that you are not able to do it. This is a difficult time to get through and a tempting time to give up. To make matters worse you sometimes seem to be going backwards and things that you could do an hour ago now totally elude you!

The next stage now begins as some learning takes place and you can feel it happening minute by minute. You concentrate carefully on one or two vital things and you take your time and achieve your first success. This is like the car driver who for the first time lets the clutch out at the right speed and the car moves forward smoothly instead of jumping three times and stalling. You may not get it right the very next time but you now know you can do something that you were previously unable to do. This stage is referred to as *conscious competence*. You know how to change the gears but you are fully conscious of what you are doing all of the time. To hold a conversation at the same time would be way past your limits. To change down a gear on the corner seems impossible. It is all you can do to remember to look in the side mirror. There is only one way from this stage to the next and that is practice. There are no short cuts, though tips given by a teacher may make your practice more effective.

The final stage of learning is what is called *unconscious competence*. You are so skilled at doing something that you cannot imagine not having being able to do it effortlessly. At this stage the skill feels part of you. The musician can think and the notes come out almost of their own accord. The car in front stops and you have hit the breaks before you have had a chance to think. You are able to ski just as easily as if you were walking down the street.

The trick is to get through the *conscious competence* stage to the *unconscious competence* stage without giving up. It helps to record your progress as that way you will see small improvements that otherwise you would forget about. By plotting the changes, you keep yourself motivated. A good teacher helps as they will pace you through the times when it all seems too much trouble for so little progress.

10

The Changing World of Work

Toys

I am not a technophobe but I had a portable computer when they were the size of sewing machines. I was into mobile phones when they cost as much as a small car, weighed as much as a concrete block and had a battery that lasted for about five calls.

Nor am I easy prey for the next gimmick. Pencil and paper has served me well over the years and I am not about to give it up for something sleek, expensive, and more difficult to use.

In the last week, I had three experiences that lead me to believe that technology and humans are marrying better than they had in the past. Firstly, I had a query about motor taxation. I was taking a fully taxed car off the road and putting an untaxed one on and I had no desire to give Charlie McCreevy 1% more than I absolutely had to. In the old days you went to the motor taxation office, took a ticket in the queue, and wasted half a day and there was nothing you could do about it.

'Try dublincity.ie', piped up a voice from across the room so I did what I was told. Up came the site and I went to the section about motor vehicles. 'Click here to contact us' it told me so I did and forgot all about it. Half an hour later, I logged on and there was a polite reply saying that they could deal with my question by e-mail but if I sent back a phone number it could be dealt with more easily. I sent my number back and lo and behold ten minutes later I get a helpful voice on the phone explaining to me exactly what I have to do. This was a good common sense service and as a taxpayer, I felt I was getting value for money. Take a bow, dublin city.ie. Forget the queues – all the forms to fill in can be printed off in the comfort of your home.

Then I was going mad in the office listening to the robot voice at the airport giving me none of the information I wanted about when a plane would arrive. Again, I was told 'Dublin airport is on the net'. Sure enough once you go to their site you may as well be in the airport. Couldn't be simpler.

Next, I was given an O2 XDA for Christmas and my inner-self

was saying that this was another gimmick and by 3 January, I would be back to bits of paper. Wrong. Technology for humans has arrived.

This gizmo, which is smaller than a pack of cards, and does everything except make scrambled egg on toast is revolutionising my life. I now have a laptop and a phone combined in the same shell in my back pocket and with enough memory to write a book and include the photographs. From now on, I will only use a pen for cheques and maintain a good writing implement as a status symbol!

I understand that this piece of equipment which has been sent to me by the gods costs around €600. It sits in a cradle beside your computer and anything you want to duplicate from your computer to it happens automatically. It can be a phone, or a hands-free phone. I can make notes in my appalling handwriting and it will turn them into typing. It does my e-mail, goes on the internet, and practically talks to me. Anything I want to beam to those near to me goes at a press of a button. No wires in a world that is increasingly filled with spaghetti. And it is all the usual things like an alarm clock and calculator. It is as easy to use as a pen and paper and if I put it in the washing-machine, it doesn't matter because all the info is on my computer.

This is the most useful thing I have got since my electric toothbrush. I am a truly happy man.

What? Your one is a GPS as well? And it reads out the e-mails to you? Wow!

Hooks of steel

When I was about 13 my mother gave a present of Dale Carnegie's famous book, *How to Win Friends and Influence People*, to a young man about to begin his working life. I thought this crass, and told her so. She told me it was the bit about making friends that was important and that it was no harm for people to think about it. I spouted back some nonsense about people liking you for yourself and the like.

My mother not only had a gift for friendship, but she was always working at it. There is rarely a month in my life when somebody I hardly know doesn't tell me of some kindness he or she remembers. As in so many things that pass between mothers and their teenage sons, she was right and I was wrong. Unfortunately, she can not hear me admit it now.

The key to friendship, according to Australian writer, Dorothy Rowe, is to reconcile our own individual way of seeing things with our need to interact with others who have their own way of seeing things. Friendship is very other centred and it is a great help to shy people to think this way. Pay attention to what *they* are saying, and not to what *you* are thinking. Then it is simple. People like being listened to. They like being looked at. They like compliments. Then they like to hear about you in moderate doses. A good guide to making friends is to assume the other person is shy and that you are trying to make them feel more comfortable.

Today the constant shortage of time is making it more difficult for people to maintain friendships and they do need maintenance in the same way as a garden does. Working hours are longer and, in the cities, it is not unusual to spend 10 hours a week in your car commuting to work. People phone each other and arrange to meet at a specified time and place and it will be cancelled if something 'more important' just has to be done. Friends don't just drop in with the ease of earlier generations. It is as if many people are deciding that they have to get the business of life over and then get back to their friendships when they retire. The garden is too much trouble so they turn it into a huge lawn. The flowers can wait until we have time.

We have reached a stage where *Coronation Street* and life blend, actors are treated as all too real, and a tabloid culture treats fiction as fact. Huge audiences get involved in this pseudo friendship instead of taking the time to sample the real thing. On top of all this is the mantra of the twentieth-first century telling us all we have to have time for ourselves!

It just cannot all fit. So increasingly, people are finding opportunities for friendship at work. Friendship comes in many forms but we all know once something is more than a casual acquaintance. Someone once said that you don't make friends, you recognise them. There is truth in that, but for it to go anywhere requires reciprocity and effort. Gradually more topics are discussed, and at a deeper level. Slowly the stage is reached where each is contributing to the other's life and it has the peculiar quality of making us feel more human.

It is not a sexual thing, but as usual, there are sex differences. People find it easier to open up to women. Men are more likely to interpret a friendly gesture from a woman as sexual. As always there are wonderful opportunities for misunderstandings. The type of friendships differs too, with women discussing feelings and men being more focused on activities together. The styles have been described as face to face versus side by side.

While a great friend may be the one who can give without any desire to receive, most of us like a two-way street. There are those who seem to do all the taking and regard it as their God-given right to criticise you to their heart's content. Back to gardening. A wise woman told me she prunes her friends each year. Some are just too high maintenance so out with the secateurs!

I was talking with a friend recently (after about 20 failed attempts to get together) and our conversation turned to the huge increase in counselling and psychotherapy and the stresses and strains of ordinary living that force people to seek help.

'What,' she wondered, 'ever happened to friends?'

Good work - if you can get it

'Good work, a job well done'. Nice praise if you receive it. A good motivator if you deliver it. But just what is good work? If a craftsman does some woodwork the quality of material, attention to detail and effort are there for all to see. It is easy to associate the pride felt with the work completed. But as we move further and further from the land, from craftsmanship, and from individual effort and skills honed over a life-time, it becomes increasingly difficult to keep that connection between excellence, effort and something that feels 'good'. In today's world, ethics and values may be slipping through the woodwork.

People do not just work for money. Well very few do! Surveys regularly show that people would still like to work rather than retire. Those who do not need the money still feel the need to be productive. Enya, U2 and Van Morrison could sit by the pool from now to eternity. But they keep working. Humans like to have an effect on the world they live in. Watch the joy an infant gets when they realise they are able to make something happen. When they learn to talk they go through the 'do it again' stage as if to convince themselves that what they do and say matters – and we never lose it.

What we do does matter, but thinking about ethical issues is not very fashionable. We are told to get real. In the 'real' world the bottom line is what matters. Even if you have to bend the rules! Television executives have to chase audiences. Even if it means dumbing down. Genetic engineers want to push the barriers, even if it means playing God. Businesses live and breathe for the quarterly results. And politicians want to keep the machinery of society greased – and their palms.

A bit cynical? Thankfully yes. The fact is that while most people do not go as far as JFK when he exhorted not to think of what your country could do for you, but the other way round, they do want to feel that what they are contributing is valuable, and in some sense that they are doing the right thing. I am still sentimental enough to enjoy Julia Roberts convincing Richard Gere to build ships rather than dismember companies in *Pretty Woman*. We all start the day looking in the mirror and we like to have some respect for what is looking back at us.

The cynics will say that the tribunals and jails are filled with people who were not troubled by the 'looking in the mirror' test. But while we start the day looking at ourselves, we continue it wanting the respect of our family, colleagues, and indeed the world at large. When a judge issues an apparently lenient sentence because a person has lost their reputation it just may show some wisdom as to the severity of punishment already suffered.

The real world is the one we create. Do we want a world where loyalty matters or can loyalty be taken too far? Does it sound antiquated when we talk of someone as being of 'good character' or have we lost something worthwhile? When we are faced with difficult choices, compromise may often be the best route – but it depends on what compromises we make!

One way of showing how we value work is by what we pay for it. So, we live in a community that thinks a lot more of lawyers than nurses and we pay all teachers the same whether they are good or bad. I wonder!

Times may be tougher, but they are paradise compared to the tough times of the 1980s. At least now, most people have work to go to. So, what would be a piece of good work today? Spot some talent and encourage it. That is good work in anyone's language, any time and any place and you can look at yourself in the mirror and feel good about it.

Working Mothers - now that's real work

Remember the last time you picked up a magazine to read a piece about working fathers. I doubt it. Fathers are supposed to work. Or a piece about the effects of female unemployment on their children. Never. Whatever the massive changes in the workforce in the last generation the old stereotypes have not moved much. A man is devastated to lose his job, or depressed and ashamed to be out of work. Some women, once they have children, are made feel guilty about working ... by society, by the Church, by their parents, by their husbands and maybe even by themselves.

In this world of sexual equality, working women still take the brunt of the second job – that is all the unpaid jobs to do with the home and children. When you combine the paid and unpaid jobs women do about half as much again as their men. This means it is harder for them to unwind because while men go home to relax, women go home to keep working. Women are not having it all. They are doing it all!

It never ceases to amaze me how a woman can co-ordinate work, different diaries for each child and her husband, school lunches, supermarket shopping without forgetting anything while also paying the television licence, sending birthday cards and thank you letters, and collecting the dry-cleaning on the way to visit Auntie Maureen in hospital. Any Pentium processor would just give up!

It is as plain as the nose on your face that most mothers are not working to have it all, but to have anything at all. All the time there is the nagging doubt about whether this is best for their children or whether it is damaging them in a myriad of psychological ways. The research of a few decades now seems to point to one conclusion. The main thing that does damage the children is the guilt the mother feels and the over-indulgent behaviour it leads her to.

Mothers working outside the home do not appear to have any effect on academic performance, good or bad. Daughters of working mothers tend to be more assertive and independent and are more likely to choose their mother as a model for the person they most admire. Sons of working mothers are more likely to develop independent living skills like cooking and ironing. If the woman enjoys both her job and home life then that is a good recipe for parent/child relationships.

About the only negative is the guilt. Mothers who feel guilty often spoil their children to make up for not 'being there for them'. Doing so is bad for their academic performance and their relationships with their friends. So, in short, it is only the guilt about working that causes the problems. Get rid of the guilt and all is well.

The key to how women cope with 'doing it all' is found in the signals they get from family friends and the larger society. If these are supportive, women not only cope but also feel greater self-esteem and pride in coping with their multiple roles. If the vibes are discouraging, they feel guilt.

The first thing a society can do to make women feel supported in their decision to have children and continue working is put a good childcare system in place. By that criterion the social support Irish women receive could only be described as miserable. Providing good childcare also means women will get further up the work pecking order. Sweden has a very good child care system, Germany much less so and how do women fare? In Sweden, most women managers have at least two children. In Germany, most are single women with no children.

Good childcare means two things. It gives working mothers public social approval. It makes the practicalities of life easier. It is the single most important change needed in the work environment for men, women and children. So, forget the guilt, and keep reminding the politicians. It is not about having it all. It is about having the essentials.

I used to be a ...

The Irish are not very good at being fired. At the moment, the very prospect is scaring the life out of the nation. Let's face it, we are only just getting used to having jobs! Now every news bulletin tells us more people are out of work and worse still, places that were as untouchable as the civil service are coming to terms with the phrase 'compulsory redundancy'. For the Irish psyche, these are real people losing jobs. The 'get rich quick, high tech dot com' phenomenon always seemed to be too good to be true so it didn't shake us to the core when that bubble burst.

What work we do determines a huge part of our self-image. How do you think of yourself? There is your job, age, sex, children, parents, friends, possessions, waistline, and accomplishments. You are an airline pilot today. Would you be just as happy as a taxi driver? Would your spouse still admire you? Could you deal with the glazed looks when you begin a sentence with 'I used to be a ...'?

Job insecurity is probably the single most important stress for employees today and a number of Swiss studies carried out in the late 1990s when mergers in the banking and pharmaceutical industry led to thousand of job losses tell us something about how people react. In short, not well. Tranquilliser use doubled. Lower back pain, a good indicator of stress, trebled. Sleep patterns were disrupted. Smoking and alcohol use increased substantially. Merely anticipating a job loss is sufficient to trigger health changes.

Surprisingly it was the best educated who had the most difficulty coping with fear of unemployment. This group, normally the healthiest workers, behave stoically, avoid missing work and postpone going to the doctor. They have more invested in their career and their self-esteem takes a greater battering. These are not people who cope well with feeling like losers.

Now a career ... what was that? It is becoming outdated and that is difficult to come to terms with if you have spent the best years of your life climbing the ladder in an organisation you identified with. The word 'career' is from the same root as 'carriage-way'.

It suggests a continuous path, moving up a hierarchy, becoming more experienced, more valued and essential to the organisation. How many jobs like that are left? The Church? The army?

Not working leaves you with time on your hands, time to think, and time to think of yourself. Contrary to popular opinion we don't think of ourselves all that much. A typical well-adjusted person only thinks about themselves 10% of the time. But that figure goes up when you are unhappy. The more self-absorbed people are the more likely they are to suffer from alcoholism, depression, anxiety and other clinical disorders.

People try to explain to themselves why things happened and we are not at all rational when we think of people who have suffered misfortune. We tend to believe that they are in some way responsible for their fate even when their predicament is caused by events completely outside their control. On some level we believe in a 'just world' and that people get what they deserve, even though this is clearly nonsense. It is as if we need a reason why 'that would not happen to me' to keep sane and happy.

We love to bask in the reflected glory of successful people. But we also cut ourselves off from 'failures' as if afraid to catch the disease. About the only value they are to us is that we can bolster our own self-esteem by making a comparison between them and us and we do this all the time. Just think about it for a while.

The vicious cycle of battered self-esteem leading to lowered expectations, less effort, high anxiety, more failure and self-blame, and even lower feelings of self-worth can be very difficult to break. But we all have a lot of control over how we present ourselves to others. Whether we are in dread of unemployment or not it is worth giving it some thought. Write down a list of things that describe how you are. Next, a list of how you feel you ought to be. Finally, a list of your ideal self.

Look at the discrepancies and do something about them. No one else will do it for you.

In love with your job

Confucius apparently said 'Choose a job that you love and you will never have to work a day in your life'. Mind you I am not sure that he said anything of the sort, or if he knew what a nine to five was, but if he did say something like that, he was on the money.

I have often said I haven't done many days' work in my life. Quite simply because most of the time it didn't feel like work. It was enjoyable, stimulating, and a lot of it I wouldn't have missed. Recently as I drove out of Dublin early one morning and saw the lanes of cars crawling to work on the other side of the carriageway I got to thinking just how awful it must be to go to work each day with a heavy heart. Can people who are trapped in that hell do anything about it?

People who enjoy their job are much less likely to get sick. When did Pat Kenny last miss a day at work? We all know the feeling of ringing a large company only to the told that the person dealing with what we want is out sick for a few days. We don't really believe it and we know that most people with the 'flu' do not have the real flu at all. People who love their work do not 'pull a sickie', but more importantly enjoying work protects us from real illness as our immune systems keep operating at full strength.

When people change job we often hear the explanation, 'My heart wasn't in what I was doing'. Many people are side-tracked before finding their ideal job and then thrive when they find something that suits them. We have all seen people who are passionate about their work. They are happier, have more energy, laugh more and stay younger.

Occupational psychologists ask 'Are you your job?' But you could stand that on its head and think more on whether the job suits your personality, lifestyle and goals. Ask yourself why are your goals your goals? Are they for you, or because of what you think society admires or your peers or family approve of. The status we get with a job dies with the job and life will feel very empty if too much of our image is tied up in our job – that is if you like the job to a degree. Let's face it life is too short to spend that many hours hating what you do. Get a job that suits the real you.

What is the real you and what is the work most suited? Try this little exercise to examine your personality and skills. Think about what you can do, and what you like to do. Imagine yourself as a brand. What is your logo? What is your slogan? What is special about you?

Think of yourself in work and having fun there. Your colleagues, and how you relate to them, are important because you may see as much of them as you do of your spouse and children. A great advantage about being yourself in your job is that you do not have to put on an act and rest assured, everyone sees through the act anyway.

Being passionate about your job does not mean becoming a workaholic. People become workaholics to fill a void or run away from relationships, family, even real life. Whereas the person who works with enjoyment and energy has the psychological luxury of being themselves 24 hours a day. The modern disease of 'presenteeism', just being at work for long hours trying to look good, is a mug's game. If you are doing it, you are storing up big psychological trouble for yourself, because acting is a stressful business. Many people treat their job like a passionless marriage. They are in it for security. To work for the money is sad. They fear change or development.

Here is another way to spend an hour if you are thinking about you and your job. Write your obituary. How would you like to be remembered by your friends, family and people at work? We all like to think that we matter, that what we do with our time, both at work and at play, makes a difference. Write a few lines and if you don't like what you see start trying to find something to do that puts more of you in your job, and less of your job in you.

It's only a few envelopes

Think of the people you work with every day. You like some, others you may not be so fond of. Some you absolutely detest. But by and large, they are a normal bunch of upstanding people, a bit like you. This morning you may have gone down to the shop, bought the paper, maybe a loaf of bread, stood in the queue and handed over €10 and probably didn't even check your change. All around you, the shelves are packed with merchandise but it would never even cross your mind to pocket something without paying. That is shoplifting. That is a crime and you could end up in jail. The very idea is preposterous.

Think back on the people in the queue at the till. Most of them wouldn't shoplift either. But how many of them would pilfer from work without it costing them a thought. Even the word pilfer makes it sound a lot softer – less of a crime and more a misdemeanour.

For companies, large and small, the goods stolen have an enormous impact on profits. In some retail businesses employees steal more than shoplifters. In the corporate world, it can knock several percentage points off earnings. Yet, the people who are doing the stealing think of themselves as fundamentally honest.

Picture the large busy office. Who would miss a few envelopes – and you are sending out the parish newsletter tonight! Many employees think nothing of putting a supply in their bags. Or it is coming near term time and the kids go though A4 lined pads at a fierce rate. 'Well I worked late three days last week so I deserve a few'. Then a handful of biros would be no harm and some batteries for the Walkman. That is before the phone is used for personal calls. This sum always staggers me.

Just one personal call is about 15 cent. So 10 a week is €1.50. Then you work 48 weeks of the year so that is €72. There are 100 people in the company so over €7,000 is gone on the phone alone and that is not counting the people who dial children in the USA and spend hours on the internet. Before long one person's salary is being spent on private phone calls and you still haven't built in the time lost when the person was not working productively.

People who routinely do the above do not think of themselves as thieves. Most of us would not consider them thieves either. Indeed, it is often described as 'innocent' pilfering. They would feel very hard done by if reprimanded. It is seen as victimless and anyway 'they can afford it'. But a proportion of employees go a good deal further and the item that mysteriously disappeared from work and had to be replaced is residing at home. Security consultants estimate that about 30% of employees do steal, and that another 60% will steal if given sufficient motive and opportunity. That does not leave a lot of honesty and integrity in the workforce.

How can companies cut down on both small-scale random theft and the more serious stealing of goods and cash? Well, the first thing is to be aware that before committing the act the employee assesses the risk. They ask themselves what is the probability of being caught and what would happen if caught. This is why the person who wouldn't dream of taking a packet of envelopes from Eason's (stealing), thinks nothing of doing it at work (everybody does it/I am entitled to it). Thieves, large and small, rationalise their behaviour by saying that they are just typical people trying to get ahead in a fundamentally dishonest world.

So company policy is important. Make the risk high. Make it clear that the behaviour is frowned upon. It works in the golf driving range where the ball is clearly marked 'Stolen From'.

Look out for signs of people being disgruntled. If people feel they are not being paid enough, or have been passed over for promotion, however justified, they lower their standards. If they do not feel valued by, and involved in, the organisation they lower them still further.

Watch out for the person who resents having their work supervised and never takes holidays.

Then there are the three B's. A disquieting number of employees turn to crime because they have financial difficulties – with babes, booze or bets.

Homework

For people who are tired of the daily commute the prospect of working from home can become very attractive. Many companies have become flexible about allowing people do some or all of their work from elsewhere and for people at various stages in their career it is an option worth considering. It conjures up images of having that extra hour in bed and shuffling down the stairs in a tracksuit, making a cup of coffee and turning on the computer or lifting the phone. How different from the alarm going off before dawn, having a shower, dressing smartly and then spending an hour in the car.

However it is not a simple as it seems and one set of statistics that I came across recently showed that about half of those who tried the option returned to the normal cut and thrust of corporate life within 18 months. What seemed like a great idea at the time just did not work out. Another study of 400 employees with a variety of companies found that those who worked from home tended to work more hours (though they had cut out the commute). More worryingly, they tended to have more family conflict than people who went to the office. The clear lines between work and home disappeared with negative results for work, home, professionalism, personal relationships and self-esteem. Whatever the precise nature of your work if you are at home you fall prey to neighbours who do not work and tempt you to do likewise. Professionalism can also suffer if there are children at home. If you are dealing with a client who hears a child being demanding in the background, you run the risk of being taken less seriously. In my case in the country, it is more usually a cow or a sheep that punctures any air of competence I may be conveying. You may be totally focused but the client may have doubts!

What people who work from home often do not take into account is that the situation does not just change for them. It also changes for everyone else who calls that space home. If you have papers all over the dining-room table they are there for all who visit the house to see. They are also there to be walked on by the cat or have coffee spilled on them. If you have clients who visit you at home, this has implications for the neatness of the areas you will use and for the behaviour of the other people in the house. These are tricky issues that the whole family needs to agree on. By working at home, you have made it a smaller and more restrictive place for the other people who share it. If possible, have a dedicated office.

The biggest difficulty for some people is that they miss the social camaraderie and gossip of the workplace. You can have many kinds of friendships with workmates that are enjoyable and feed a range of interests that are not available at home. Not all people are good at the amount of solitude working at home can bring. This is particularly so if they are desk bound. A lot of your own company can make you feel very isolated from the real world.

So, if you are contemplating the move you should think about a few things. Firstly, satisfy yourself that you have the space in your house to work there without hugely interfering with the other people who live there. Put in extra phone lines so that you know what is work and what is not. Then you have to keep clear distinctions between work and family life. Children may resent that you are in the house but not available to them and you have to work out with them how best to handle this. Clearly one of the advantages of working from home is closer contact with the family, but you have to work out how to avoid turning the potential benefit into a problem.

Your change of how you work also has implications for your neighbours. If people are visiting your house regularly that is more traffic and noise for them and more times their gate is blocked! Think how you would feel and behave accordingly.

Then there is the toughest thing of all. Having the self-management abilities to get started and do what needs to be done when it needs to be done so that you and those close to you can enjoy the benefits of the extra hours in the day and reduced stress in your life.

As good as your last job

'You are only as good as your last job' is a phrase that has been around for a long time. But I seem to hear it more and more. As the world of work becomes increasingly freelance and contract-based often the only job security people have is their reputation and track record. This is not just a standard placed on workers by employers. No, it occurs regularly in advertisements for all kinds of services. People put up their website demonstrating their wares and invite you to contact their list of satisfied customers. At first glance, this looks like a fine example of people setting high standards, policing them and maintaining them. If you are a customer, there is nothing wrong with that.

What interested me was the psychological effect of using this mantra as the criterion by which you wish to be judged. In searching for answers I came across one of those thousands of religious sites on the web that often have some interesting nuggets nestling in among the propaganda. This man was expressing the view that the Christian Churches do not seem to have any philosophy around work today to guide the believer as to what is the appropriate way to integrate work into life. He had a point. We can spot other people letting work dominate their lives, but not ourselves. This was in my mind when I bumped into a well-paid semi-state benchmarked employee who I assumed enjoyed the security of the job, got in plenty of golf, spent quality time with his family and basically was on the pig's back compared to the 'real world'. What was the one word, I asked, that he would use to describe his work now. He didn't have to think long. 'Unrelenting', was the word he used, before adding 'you're only as good as your last job, you know. Then there is the fear that someone will point out to you that you're not even as good as your last job any more and that means some Siberia will be your lot before too long in this organisation!'

Unrelenting is a harsh word to apply to a significant section of your life. If you described your marriage as unrelenting, you would be on your way to a counsellor before long. As we continued the conversation, he told me that the last project he had managed was the most challenging one he had ever undertaken. The one before that was the next hardest. Once you get a reputation for getting it done right the bar gets higher. The only thing you can do is keep succeeding. Or fail and if you fail, no one remembers the long track record. No. They just know 'yer man' isn't what he used to be.

Experience grows, but the bar also gets higher and the pressure grows. This type of climate can encourage a cynical management to focus on the 5% that wasn't satisfactory and ignore the 95% that was. So, you have people waking up at 4 am in fear and doubt about their current project and likely to write notes about it during Christmas dinner. Work and the rest of life have blended into one. Managed well this may not be a bad thing. The car dealer who gets you interested in a new motor on the golf course certainly didn't feel like he was working and it didn't ruin his game one bit. But the creative advertising copywriter who always has the next campaign in mind and is jotting down snippets of conversation all the time will require a tolerant spouse, family and friends.

If you found yourself saying 'your family life is only as good as the last weekend with the kids' you would know immediately just how stupid a concept it was. But it just might help you focus on the many things in life that matter. Quality of work is one thing. Quality of life is another thing altogether.

11

Change – The Only Stability There Is

Routines and ruts

The clocks have gone forward. There are buds on the trees. The buzz of the lawn-mower is back on the weekends. Change is in the air and there is new life everywhere. Some of our routines are going to be replaced by new ones and it is always a good time of the year to see if any of our once cherished routines have become ruts that we could well do with climbing out of. Life is for living and some sage once pointed out that the difference between a rut and a grave is only about six feet!

Life is so busy that to just get things done we need the world to be predictable. But if we don't keep an eye on ourselves, it is all too easy to wander through whole weeks in a bit of a trance. You get in the car and go to work. Can you remember anything you saw on the way? The radio was on in the car. Most of it went in one ear and out the other. You read the paper and nothing sinks in. You go to the same pub with the same people on the same night of the week. Do you all feel refreshed by it? Are your worlds getting more interesting or shrinking? Maybe it is time for a jolt to the system. Do what Christy Moore says in 'Lisdoonvara'– 'Climb that mountain or jump in that lake'.

It is a very easy thing to open your eyes and take a new look at the world. It is surprising what a few small changes will do for you. Go to work a different route. Or maybe walk. When you walk down the street look at the second storeys of the shops. They are much more interesting. Tune the radio to a different station. Buy a CD from a part of the shop that you never went into before. Read a different magazine and order a drink that you haven't tasted for years.

Like most men, I don't have a very full understanding of why a visit to the hairdresser gives such a boost to a woman's confidence. Then I look around at the legions of dull grey creatures and ask myself does life have to look so dull? It is time to cull the wardrobe. But try as I might my background comes to haunt me.

I come from one of those homes that didn't buy jam. You made it. Or rather my mother did. As I look at a jacket I will never wear again I can hear myself returned to conversations overheard in childhood as if it were yesterday. They ran something like this – 'Do you think I would get another summer out of that blue cotton dress. I've got three summers out of it now. I made it myself, you know'.

Yes. We know. The entire world could see that. While I am a prudent person who still admires all those values, there is another part of me screaming to throw out three-quarters of what is in my wardrobe and reinvent myself just that little bit.

We need enough routine to give structure to our lives to allow ourselves be curious and creative about the things that matter. But once that routine starts to become a straitjacket, it is time to cry halt.

The old cliché – a change is as good as a rest – is probably true. And me? I decided to spend some time on an uninhabited island. *Treasure Island* is about as far as you can humanly get from routine!

School for life

Year after year, people sign up for night classes. Not everyone stays the course. The spirit may be willing but the flesh is sometimes weak. If you have a busy job, or a busy family, finding the time and energy to make an extra commitment at night-time and weekends is a big obligation.

Every now and again, we make a special effort, but let's be honest most of us did not learn to speak French, or lose weight, cook better, get up early, reorganise the garden, or become a campaigner for the improvement of society. No, most of us have stepped back into being ourselves with the pattern much as it was before.

Learning something new is one of the greatest confidence-builders you can find. For a start, you usually find out that you possess many skills that you have never identified as skills. Women, in particular, tend to under-value just how much they do in running a household – probably enough to manage a small business! But they do not see it that way. We are all caught inside our own bubble of reality.

Take learning to paint for example. I grew up in an era when you were not even allowed to try your hand with a paintbrush unless you showed you had 'talent'. That is, the school would only teach you if you didn't need to be taught, and for the rest there was no point in teaching you because art couldn't be taught. It was a talent, not a skill.

Years later I go into houses where people proudly display their latest watercolour, and these are people who (and I mean no disrespect) are every bit as untalented as I am. But a few simple rules got them started and interested teachers soon helped them to do passable work. All were well satisfied with the results and continued improvements, and rightly so. Some were bitten by the bug and were developing interests and aspects of their personality that they were previously unaware of.

Music and singing are two more from the talent stable. But

again, practice and teaching can enable anyone to develop their skills to levels that they never even contemplated. They will hear parental echoes telling them 'you'll be sorry when you are older that you didn't practise'. Lots of us are – but it is never too late.

Learning a new skill is a good way to get some time for yourself, time that has nothing to do with work, family or friends. Indeed you will probably make new friends and it is always very reassuring to discover that people you never met before positively enjoy your company – another good confidence-builder.

New expertise keeps us ready to look at everyday life in different ways. The person who does interior design looks at houses with a new eye. New knowledge keeps us fresh, vital and alive. Without it, we don't just stand still – we shrink a little every day.

Anyone who writes regularly is well used to people asking how they come up with ideas all the time. The answer lies somewhere between facing a blank page and feeling a deadline looming. The plain fact is that most people given half an hour to write a few paragraphs about something that interests them will make a better stab at it than they thought they would. Observing and describing the world gives you new eyes with which to see the world. Ask anyone who keeps a diary. To do something that will be read by others sharpens the experience. Do it with a guitar and three chords and before long, it is a song.

Valuable personal change for most people just takes the commitment to hone their existing skills or acquire new ones. From then on, it is a matter of perspiration. Inspiration is a bit over-rated I think. We may get a spark of an idea and call it inspiration. But the room will not paint itself and the song will not write itself – that is the perspiration bit. It is the bit that lets you find out lots about yourself that you never even suspected.

Taking the package

'How are things?' I asked a friend of many years as he showed me around his garden with pride. This was one of the most beautiful places in Dublin to spend a summer evening at a barbecue with a glass of wine.

'Fine. There's a package going at our place and I'm going to take it and do something for myself,' he replied. He had been selling insurance since he left school and was just approaching his fiftieth birthday. We sat down on a bench and he told me his plans. He loved gardening. He was good at it. He had taken courses in it. Many people had the money to pay him to keep their garden in the same condition as he kept his own. He would keep his work-load at the level he felt most comfortable with. The mortgage was paid and his wife worked in a job that she loved, so why should he spend one more day driving in to a job that had become routine and a drudge? He looked happy, excited and invigorated as he told me this.

The pattern of work through life is changing. In 1900 two-thirds of men over 65 were still working. Today's figure is down to 16% of men and only 7% of women. People want to leave their job before getting the bus pass for a variety of reasons. They are bored with doing the same thing. They want to spend more time with their family, or partaking in sports or hobbies. Increasingly they want to do something they like doing and to be paid for it.

Families often dovetail well. At the age when men may be wanting to take it easier women who have been out of the workforce while raising children are eager to go back to full-time work. With mortgages paid and children reared, many people are in a financial position to take a little risk.

It may be the coffee shop you have always wanted to open. It may be the immaculate dry stone walls you like building. Whatever it is the chances are that the pleasure gained will give you a spring in your step that was gone in your old job. People who have worked for large companies derive great satisfaction from 'working for myself at long last'.

Work is so important to our self-esteem that the all or nothing cut off point at 65 is probably the stupidest system we could design. Large companies are beginning to realise this and are introducing structured withdrawal for a number of years before retirement day. That way a person can work less, while still giving the company the value of their experience.

But many workers now vote with their feet and once the sums add up and they see that they can make ends meet, they are gone. What people do after they retire tells us a lot about the psychology of work. To be doing something is a deep psychological need and there is the social aspect to work which is very important to people. Increasingly people are not going to retire at all. But what they will do is change to part-time work and gradually withdraw from the full-time commitment that characterises their work pattern from 20 to 50.

There are many middle-aged people around who still regret that they didn't play in a band. If you are one of those people who still do air guitar in the privacy of the shower, enjoy wearing jeans and wish you were young enough for them to be leather, then you know how important it is to seize the moment and do what you really want.

It is one thing to have regrets at 50. It must be horrible to have them at 65. So, make that change while enough cylinders are still firing.

A new start

There was time when people who were lucky enough to have a job, clung on to it for dear life. It didn't have to be fulfilling. It didn't have to be uplifting. It just had to be done and it paid the bills. It used to be said of Guinness, once a massively influential employer in Dublin, that they looked after their employees and families from the womb to the tomb.

These days are no more. Few jobs in the private sector can now be thought of as secure. The big social pressure not to change – 'how could you give up the security of that job? Are you mad?' – is no more. People may lose their job which is very stressful. Or they may actively seek a different job and being successful in that quest brings with it a different set of stresses.

Deciding to look for a new job is one of life's big decisions yet people usually do not give it the thought it deserves and will only rarely seek professional advice. People will happily, well maybe not, fork out money to pay legal or medical bills, or to keep the car in proper order, but would not contemplate spending a penny seeking advice about how or if to change job, or what type of work they are best suited to.

A good start is to do an assessment of how you feel about your present job. I am a great believer in lists and this is a two-list exercise. To begin write down everything that you are unhappy about in your present job. This can be as all-embracing as 'not feeling challenged enough' or as minor as the colour of the walls. Take half an hour and think through your typical week and what you do not like about it.

Once you have that done divide what you have written into two columns and have a good look at what you find. In column one lists all of the things that are specific to the particular place where you are now working. It will include location, atmosphere, personalities, etc. In column two, list all of the things that are specific to the job you do and that would apply no matter where you did the job. So, do you want a change of career or a change of location? This is a good time to ask yourself how you got to your current position. Was it planned, or lucky, or maybe even an accident?

If you do decide to move, take time to do your research properly because you can easily jump from the frying pan into the fire. You may need to do an additional course to prepare yourself. You will need to do some research about opportunities and you must prepare a good CV. Crucially you need to assess the implications for the other members of your family. Might you have to move house? You are not the only one involved!

When you get the call offering you the new job you may enter a strange psychological space for a while. You may begin to talk the options over with trusted friends and it is as if you are trying to talk yourself out of the new challenge. For a time the security and familiarity of your current job take on an enhanced attractiveness. You may even feel a loyalty to your present colleagues and will certainly feel apprehension about the new job. If you have done your preparatory work well and considered your situation fully then it is time to face the situation. Make the move.

Then three simple things will help. *One*, give yourself time to learn the ropes. No one expects you to know everything immediately. *Two*, irrespective of how you came to your new position give it 100%. *Three*, get to know people – even if you feel like eating lunch alone, don't.

Put all the experience you have into a mental drawer because at first you may feel you know nothing relevant to the new job. Gradually you will find yourself going to that 'drawer' where there is something useful for you to contribute. If all goes well in about six months, you will find that all the contents of that mental drawer have been integrated into your new worklife.

Hopefully you will feel the better for it.

12

Recharge the Batteries

Feeling under the weather?

The plan is simple. You work all year round but it is worth it because you can look forward to two sunny weeks in the summer with your family and then return to work with your batteries recharged.

We know that holidays are not all plain sailing. For many people they are stressful times when household friction, that can survive small amounts of time together, boils over. They are also emotional times as people reflect on their own childhoods and families and compare their current situation to the idyll of the better summers we all had as youngsters when we can scarcely remember a cloud in the sky! We invest a lot emotionally in holidays and we count on them too much to compensate for the rest of the year. So, it is normal to feel a bit let down and sad on returning to work after the annual break.

In Ireland, we have the additional factor of our weather, where the only thing that is predictable about it is that it is unpredictable, and frequently inclement. Since the 1980s it has become commonplace to talk of SAD, or seasonal affect disorder. Many people feel depressed, some quite seriously, as the short days of winter and lack of sunlight come in on them. How it works, no one is sure. Estimates are that in our latitude up to 10% experience SAD to some degree and that it is related to daylight is beyond question. First of all it is doesn't really happen until you live 30 degrees from the equator. Secondly, it occurs only in the months of little sunlight. Most importantly, the effects can be reversed either by daylight, or by artificial devices which mimic the effects of sunlight. To be effective the light is at least five times stronger than a well-lit office, about as bright as a spring morning on a clear day.

SAD is four times as common in women for some reason, and the figure I always rely on is that about 1% of the residents of Florida suffer it to some degree and as you go north this figure increases to about 10% in Alaska. Well as far I am concerned, we share more with Alaska most years!

January and February have never been my favourite times of

the year. Unless I get away from Ireland to either the sun or the snow, that is. In the days when I had something approximating a 'real' job, I used to hate going to work in the dark and going back to the car park in the dark for eight or more long weeks. Since my worklife is now a great deal more varied, I have been surprised to find that the winter blues are far less a feature than they used to be. This is probably a mixture of variety in worklife and actually seeing some daylight on a regular basis. There is a story, probably apocryphal, that there was once a proposal to build an underground tunnel from the car park in MIT to the university proper so that people would be sheltered from the snow and rain during the year. Apparently, it was vetoed because some of the hard working engineers and computer scientists could go the year round without seeing daylight! For many people in Ireland during winter the only light they see is the office lighting and one wonders can this possibly be a good way to live. Those who are out and about still get adequate sunlight even on the shortest day, 21 December. But many people now spend their days cooped up in modern buildings with artificial light. People will say that they cannot get out for a half-hour walk in the middle of the day. But from what I see smokers are able to get out for a 10-minute break several times a day. Maybe the irony of it is that that the blast of daylight they are getting is doing them as much good as the ciggie is doing them harm!

The weather and the seasons do have a big effect on our health. Mammals begin to eat more as the days get shorter and we are mammals and we put on a few pounds each winter. Hospitals know that if you have a cold snap in winter there will be an increase in heart attacks about three days later, strokes a few days later and then serious respiratory problems next.

SAD is now a recognised sub-section of what we know of as depression but apart from its time-based nature it is different in many ways from other types of depressive illness. The person with SAD sleeps more than usual and eats more than usual as well as having decreased energy. This craving for sweet foods usually results in weight gain. They feel very fatigued and have difficulty carrying out their normal routine. Sometimes they are tense and find it difficult to tolerate any stress, they may be irritable and avoid social contact, have less interest in sex, and generally feel miserable, guilty and have low self-esteem.

While most of us do not suffer from SAD, and I don't think I ever did – more a dose of winter-time blues combined with back to work – it is probably worth our while to learn a little from those who do. In humans melatonin – a sleep-related hormone – is produced in greater levels in the dark and there is evidence that this hormone causes symptoms of depression. So, it behoves us all to look at how we live during these winter months.

So what to do about it. Take a few long weekends if you can. If the weather forecast is good on Thursday night be ready to head off like a bat out of hell at lunch-time on Friday. For companies this might be the only time absenteeism will pay off in the longer term.

Take a walk during lunch-time instead of sitting indoors with a cup of coffee and a sandwich. Exercise really is a bit of a cure all.

Ease off the booze and have a few early nights which brings me to my own secret weapon for fighting the blues. As a child, my grandmother always told me about the dawn chorus – and it infuriated me that I never woke up in time to hear it. For many years, it was one of life's mysteries. But no more. Once spring arrives I am up at 5.30 am. Lots of people cope with feeling a bit down by staying up late watching television and not getting up until mid-day. That only makes them worse!

Remember it is normal to feel sad now and again. It is a human reaction to loss of something important. People experience sadness about all sorts of typical life experiences – not getting a job, moving away from friends, a pet dying, relationship difficulties – and these feelings are not forms of depression or SAD. Rather they are the stuff of life that we go through and come out the other side.

So, set the alarm clock. Get out in the garden and sit down with your cup of tea. Sure, you might even have time to walk to work. If a small percentage of you get to appreciate the habit of early rising, I am convinced the world will be a better place!

So, if you are feeling under the weather maybe you should get out in it more!

Jet lag - don't fly too high

Oh the excitement of it all. The first time you get on an aeroplane in the course of your work. You are going to foreign shores and someone else is paying. Soon the novelty wears off which is why the airlines spend a lot of money massaging the egos of the business traveller in return for their loyalty.

You can tell the people who travel a lot. They are the ones drinking water when the bar is free. Then they are either working or asleep for the duration of the flight. I travel regularly but not enough to go on the water. No, my transatlantic routine is a meal and a few Bacardi and Cokes or Bloody Marys (neither of which I ever drink on the ground), a bit of work that I can tidy up later and a good sleep. That is why I get jet lag and am determined to mend my ways!

Jet lag is a very real phenomenon experienced by over 90% of long-haul travellers. Our bodies are used to the circadian rhythm of a 24 hour clock and take time to adjust to major time shifts. Fatigue and irritability are the main symptoms, combined with a general mental fuzziness that makes you go back, check three times if you locked your hotel room, and then go to a meeting without the essential file. Then at the business meeting it is typical to have difficulty concentrating. Many people experience a total lack of motivation for anything that requires effort or skill. Put a stomach upset on top of all that, and about half long-haul travellers do, and I think you will agree that it is worth doing something to avoid jet lag. So here are a few tips.

Firstly, you should plan as if you will have some jet lag and do not schedule an important meeting at a time when it is very predictable that you will not be at your best.

Make sure you get a good night's sleep the night before you travel. Many people say they will catch up on their sleep on the plane. No, you won't. You will just suffer more at the other end.

Never get on a plane with a hangover. You are already dehydrated and will get further dehydrated as you travel. Ideally, it is better not to drink the night before. While in the air remember that alcohol is two or three times more potent than it is on the ground.

When you get on the plane set your watch to your destination time and begin to think in that time zone. Walk around the plane during the trip and drink a glass of water every hour. Water is the most important liquid to minimise jet lag.

Having slept, one of the best ways to get yourself going is to experience the full bright early morning sunlight. It lifts the spirits and gets you off on the best foot.

On a lighter note, air travel is fraught with class structure and I was recently victim of a wonderful humiliation. I was travelling to Heathrow. I paid no attention whatsoever to the ticket and was pleasantly surprised to be in row four with a little yellow anti-macassar on my seat to absorb the Brylcreem. The all-important curtain that divides the people from the failures was behind me!

I sat and watched as the ordinary people filed passed and made their way to the back of the plane rather in the manner I look at 1995 Japanese imports at the traffic lights. I had settled into the glow of being appreciated when there was a flurry of activity around our generously apportioned row of seats.

Could row four please stand up? A steward opened a bolt, put his delicate hip to the row of seats, and reduced them to sardine size. Then another bout of activity as the curtain behind us was taken down. We watched, shrinking in our seats, as it was re-hung in front of us, and pulled closed in front of our noses. I can now tell you to the millimetre how small an embarrassed person can become in an airline seat. I will remember to my dying day the chuckle from behind!

For future reference, could they please count the number of posh people on the plane before they let anyone on and spare decent people this embarrassment?

As I said, the novelty soon wears off!

Holidays – take your time

We need security and stability. We need change and novelty. The pendulum swings all through our lives. Too little change and we get bored, and perhaps boring. Too much change, or the wrong change, and we get anxious.

This brings me to holidays. A change is as good as a rest? Well there are probably plenty of people who gratefully returned to work after a Christmas of family rows and bickering who wouldn't agree. Christmas is one of those few times when a family who are used to cohabiting have to actually live together for nearly two weeks. Rest assured you are not alone.

Already the ads are making you feel guilty if you aren't planning a summer holiday. Do holidays matter? Yes they do, and people are becoming increasingly aware of it. Americans are well known for taking short vacations and looking down their noses at Europeans who think nothing of taking all of August off. But they are changing.

I recently spent two weeks in California where time and again I heard people say they had enough money but not enough time off. People used to boast about how long it was since they had taken a proper holiday. Now that is being seen as macho nonsense. One long-term study of over 10,000 men aged between 35 and 57 found that those who took annual holidays were 21% less likely to die over the 16 years of the study, and 32% less likely to die of heart disease.

Enter the holiday as stress-buster supreme. So how does one go about making sure that the holiday refreshes, recharges, and maybe even rejuvenates?

First of all a holiday is a time when you get away from work, not merely from the place where you go to work. Many people fall into the trap of thinking that things cannot go on without them. So, they worry about work and phone in to check their messages. It may sound like a stereotype but I have sat by a pool while the children swim, their mothers read books and the fathers take conference calls on their mobile phones. In between going up to reception to check for faxes. Turn off the phones. They will get on fine at home without you!

How did you feel your first day back at work after Christmas? Did you find it hard to settle back in? If the answer is 'yes' then good, you had a bit of a holiday. If re-entry isn't hard, you haven't been away.

You have two main choices – the restful, recharge your batteries holiday, or the stimulating, new experience, get away to foreign parts version. Think about what you want, and if you want a rest, you need to be able to know what you actually find restful. There is no point in going to some 'Bounty Bar' beach if you spend the first week recovering from the hassles of travel and the second week worrying about facing it all again. In between complaining about the food!

Many people enjoy a degree of ritual about their holidays. They return to the same place and switch gear the moment they arrive. They meet people they only see in that place each year, and yet these friendships become important and after about a week they feel the benefits. You don't slow down fully instantly. It takes a full week to relax, so if you are able to take a three-week holiday, do it. You will find it is about ten times better than the traditional fortnight.

Then there are those who want challenges in their time away from a routine worklife. These holidays are supposed to be stressful. You want to be stretched. If the aim is to disconnect from work of whatever type then it is hard to beat being pushed to the limits in some new adventure or sport. When you are going down a ski slope faster than you want there is no way your mind is anywhere other than on your immediate problem. It occurred to me the other day that if you could bring the same level of concentration to golf your handicap would drop in leaps and bounds. But I digress.

As to finding something that satisfies everybody in the family? Come on. That's a bit hard. I don't think even Disneyland have that one cracked!

13

Thinking Outside the Box

Emotional leaders – Daniel Goleman

A few years back Daniel Goleman wrote a book called *Emotional Intelligence* which quickly managed that all important cross-over from the psychology bookshelves to the everybody bookshelves. His idea was simple. We are all familiar with the intelligence we use to do mental arithmetic, solve complicated puzzles and remember vast amounts of information. People with this kind of intelligence do very well in exams. But Goleman made the case for another type of intelligence, the ability to read other people's emotions and deal with our own effectively and argued that to get on in life this emotional intelligence is a great deal more useful than traditional IQ. Anyone who has dealt with highly qualified medics or lawyers who know their field back to front but have the social and communication skills of a robot will know he was on to a good idea.

Now Goleman and his team have taken the idea further with a book that anyone who works with people will enjoy reading. For *The New Leaders* they studied nearly 4,000 executives to identify the type of leaders who are effective in managing organisations – that is people. Surprise, surprise, the traditional demanding sergeant major approach came last by a long shot.

According to Goleman the fundamental task of leaders is to 'prime good feeling' in those they lead, and this positivity brings out the best in people. Leaders manage meaning for a group, giving a way to interpret a situation and a guide as to how to react emotionally to any given set of circumstances. So, people work better *and* they feel better about it. At root then, he argues, the fundamental job of leadership is emotional in nature. The other side is that toxic leaders poison the atmosphere right through the workplace.

The emotionally intelligent leader is strong in four crucial areas –

1. *Self-awareness* – without recognising our own emotions we will be poor at managing ourselves, and less able to understand the

importance of emotion for other people. Being emotionally aware helps us develop the empathy that makes people we mix with feel understood.

2. *Self-management* – and if you cannot manage yourself what chance have you with others?

3. *Social awareness* – in short being attuned to other people, recognising fear, or anger, boredom, anxiety, or good humour. If they are laughing, so should you be.

4. *Relationship management* – a set of skills that guide the tone of the group if the person first has some of the other three awareness and management skills. The good relationship manager can sense the emotions and interests of other people and can 'read' the vibes and politics of a situation well.

With this armoury of skills Goleman identifies four very effective management styles – Visionary, Coaching, Affiliative and Democratic. Two further styles should be avoided like the plague – Pacesetting and Commanding.

The visionary leader gives people a sense of where the enterprise is going, and why, and moves them in that direction. This type of leadership is based on a shared dream that all can buy into. This is an important type of personality to have in someone who is changing the culture of an organisation.

The coaching type of leader is good at helping people identify their strengths and weakness and using their abilities to move towards agreed goals. They are good at recognising initiative and delegating to those people.

Affiliative leaders focus on the emotional needs of employees more than on their work goals. Their ability to empathise keeps people happy and they work better. They just take it for granted the person is able to do the job and try to motivate in other ways.

Democratic leaders create the sense that they really want to hear employee's thoughts. They are good listeners.

Each of the above styles builds what he calls 'resonance', that is good feeling which promotes more good feeling. By contrast, there is the pressure put on by pacesetters and commanders. It may work for a short while, but that is all.

The first four styles of leadership all translated in higher profits and a far higher proportion of key people staying with the company. People who are happy in a company are far less likely to leave, even for more money.

One final thing. Good leaders laugh more. Is the sound of laughter a familiar one during your daylight hours?

The lies we tell ourselves –
Steve Chandler

I always enjoy 'wasting' a few hours in American bookshops. There is no facet of life that isn't catered for and even in the most respectable places there are shelves full of titles that make me shift uneasily from one foot to the other in case one of my old schoolteachers just happens to be in the same shop as me 8,000 miles away and a generation later.

I can always get a good hour out of the 'self-improvement' section which is made up of recycled ideas, things to appeal to every faddist in town, absolute nonsense and the occasional gem. Motivational writer Steve Chandler is responsible for a gem I picked up recently entitled *Seventeen Lies that are holding you back and the truth that will set you free* published by that humble imprint, Renaissance Books!

So here are a few of the whoppers that you can try for size. 'I'd love to do that but I just don't have the time'. You can fool yourself with that one for a long time. Try saying it this way instead. 'I've often said I would like to do that but I don't have the commitment'. It doesn't sound very good that way, does it? But it is probably a great deal more accurate Not getting something done is rarely about time. It is usually about focus.

Here's another porkie from Mr Chandler. 'It is who you know'. Wrong. That is just an excuse. Most times, it is what you know, or what you are able to do that matters. Who you know won't be very interested in the absence of your being useful at something or other. *It is all about what you do with what you know.* How did U2, Roy Keane, Tommy Tiernan, Roddy Doyle, Padraic Harrington and Enya get where they are? Talent and hard work, and the determination to dust themselves off after hard knocks. It certainly had little or nothing to do with who they knew. But it is always a handy excuse to avoid getting out there and doing something.

Another one I liked was 'that is just the way I am'. How often have we heard that one? It usually carries the implication that you either like me the way I am or not at all. We make excuses for not talking to somebody because we are shy. We sit back because we are not a pushy type of person. Over the years, we give ourselves all sorts of personal characteristics to excuse ourselves for not doing things. I've said it before. To a large extent, how you are is how you choose to be. It is your own personal straitjacket of fear that you feel comfortable in. Go on that way if you like. But stop lying to yourself that it is part of what you are.

Another closely related one nailed by Steve Chandler is 'the longer I have a habit the harder it is to break'. Nonsense, but comforting nonsense. Ex-smokers will tell you that it only takes a second to make the decision not to smoke, and to describe oneself as a non-smoker. It is the same for someone who has been smoking for two years or 20 years. It is just a change in self-perception so that the new non-smoker replaces the old smoker. Likewise, it doesn't matter how long you have been a couch potato. After seven days of walking around the block a new way of life is getting firmly ingrained.

Which brings me to the daddy of them all – 'everything would be fine if I won the Lotto'. Money is not the source of all evil, but unearned money may well be. So if you are sitting there thinking all of your problems would be solved if your numbers came up it is probably time for you to realise that you have become very adept at self-deception. Time to cop on and get a life.

Seeing with our brain - Ian Robertson

People often ask me for a good psychology book and occasionally one comes my way. Over the last week, I have been reading *The Mind's Eye* (Bantam Press) and it has some local links. The author is Ian Robertson, professor of psychology at Trinity College Dublin, a man who has spent his career furthering understanding of what the many different parts of our brains do.

Our brains have one hundred billion cells, each with a thousand connections which work out at one hundred thousand billion cell-meeting points. Not that you would think it with some people we all know. Robertson, like many people, believes that we could get a lot more value from our brains. The book's subtitle – *The essential guide to boosting your emotional, mental and physical powers*, while a bit over the top, gives an idea of his approach.

We have five senses. We see, hear, feel, smell and taste. But there does not have to be anything present for us to experience sensation. As Ian Robertson points out, we can do all of these things at will in our mind's eye. But could we get more use from this inner power. Children are very much in touch with their senses, but as we learn language, we remove ourselves further and further into being verbalisers rather than visualisers.

Are you verbal or visual? This simple test will give you an idea. Imagine a loved one. Now imagine their face, head and shoulders. Next, a characteristic pose, then walking and then finally see them in some typical clothing. How easy did you find it?

When we cultivate imagery in the mind's eye, we use parts of our brain that are not triggered with words. Try this. What is the capital of Ireland? The word 'Dublin' jumps into your mind. No pictures. Now ask yourself to remember an important family event – a wedding, a christening, moving house. Pictures, sounds, even smells may flood into your brain. There is a big difference between the two types of memory. But in this book, you learn how to enrich memory by boosting your visual system

Words cloud the mind's eye. According to Robertson, if people talk while they taste it greatly reduces the brain's ability to tell wines apart. So much for television tasting.

But vivid imagery can have drawbacks and one of the concerns is that of having false memories. These may be benign, or devastating as in the case of abuse remembered which in some cases did not occur. Strongly visual people can be facilitated under certain conditions to 'remember' things that never happened. Robertson offers interesting insight.

I have a very clear memory of my father slamming the car door on my finger accidentally when I was five or six. I can still feel the pain and see the bone exposed through the cut flesh. Just as if it were yesterday. I still have the scar. Only thing is, it never happened. Yes, I caught my finger in the door, but he spotted me in time. I was fine after an ice cream. The scar was done with a penknife years later and I have a much dimmer memory of that.

On the positive side, top athletes get good value out of visualising events, from a two-foot putt to a marathon, before doing them. Our mental muscles seem to remember these muscular rehearsals. It is comforting to know that mental training, even if lying in bed, produces results.

Many medics are now realising the value of assisting good visualisation to reduce pain, and more importantly to give the immune system a boost with diseases from herpes to cancer. But Robertson cautions that the real 'magic bullet' for cancer will come from molecular medicine and not psychology.

To finish he takes us through his thinking on the science versus religion debate. Stimulating stuff.

Outro

Television addict - in recovery

All work and no play make Jack a dull boy. Our leisure time is vital to replenish our energies and to widen our interests in life and give free rein to the more playful parts of our personalities. But how do we spend our leisure time? The world over more and more people are doing the same thing. Since the first fuzzy pictures a little more than 50 years ago, watching television has become the world's most popular leisure pastime. After sleeping and working, we spend more time watching television than anything else. Someone said a television is a device you can sit in front of and watch people doing the things you could be doing if you weren't sitting there watching them do it. From 7 pm to 9 pm, people can live on a diet of soap from *Emmerdale* and *Eastenders* to *Fair City* and *Coronation Street* and many people do just that for two hours. Television doesn't require literacy or mobility. It has become the junk food of the mind.

I have a split personality when it comes to television. It has put bread on my table for many years and I enjoy making programmes. I watch a reasonable amount of what is on, surfing from the superb Robert Winston series on childhood to absolute dross like *Jackass*. Like many people, I find it impossible not to look at the screen even if there is an interesting conversation going on in the room. With constantly changing pictures television is a magnet for human attention. As our species evolved it was always important to be attentive to changes in the environment so we are wired to attend to changes in vision and sound.

The bad part of television is related to its addictive nature. Most of us watch too much of it. The middle-class in particular feel guilty that they watch too much. There is nothing wrong with the escapism, entertainment, stimulation and even information that television provides. But it does not seem to be good for our mood if we watch too much of it. Over three hours a day is considered heavy usage and many people do that. In surveys about 10% of people describe themselves as addicts, usually about half say they would like to cut down and with teenagers that figure is nearer to three-quarters. But despite this, hardly anybody does cut down on this massively dominant leisure activity. We turn on the television when we want to watch a particular programme, and when we are sad, lonely, bored, worried and need a bit of distraction. It works very quickly. Soon we are relaxed and relatively content. But that sense of relaxation ends when we switch off and unlike other activities such as reading a book or playing a game of cards, we do not seem to be energised by the television. Rather having viewed an hour or more of television, you are passive and less alert. You just don't have much get up and go. It hardly ever improves your humour. Heavy viewers – those who view three or more hours – become more tense, irritable and sad. They also experience a feeling of having little control over their lives. For such people life becomes a downward emotional spiral of work, sleep and television and their enjoyment of life is greatly curtailed.

There have been many experiments when people try to give up television and the results point to the nature of the addiction. Only a handful of families last longer than a few days and by that time the atmosphere in the house has usually become intolerable. You are dependent on something when you spend a great deal of time doing it or using it, do it more than you intend or want, make efforts to cut down, give up other family, social or work activities to do it, and feel withdrawal symptoms if it is not available.

So ask yourself is television one of your many important and fulfilling leisure activities? Or are you a bit of an addict and what are you going to do about it? Mark out the programmes in the paper that you would like to watch. You will probably find that the greater the difference between those choices and what you actually end up doing, the greater the guilty feeling and the lower your mood. Yet another thing we love turns out to be bad for us if we over-indulge!

Conscious work, or automatic pilot

Most of us are awake and about the place for 16 or so hours a day. Up to half of those hours will be spent at work. But just how conscious are we as we go through the day? Just how aware are we of what we are doing, thinking and feeling and of why we are doing what we are doing?

Driving to work it is easy to fall into a semi-trance, only to be jerked back to awareness by the brake lights on the car in front. All too often on my way to Dublin I find myself wondering have I gone through Carlow or not. Carlow is not an easy place to miss but we all know the feeling, and we all know that we spend large portions of the routine aspects of our day with little conscious input.

This came to mind in a queue in a large DIY shop last week. I waited in line and my turn came. The checkout woman began scanning my goods when the phone rang. She said 'excuse me', politely, and took the call and proceeded to spend five minutes assisting a customer on the phone while I was left kicking my heels. She then finished the call, smiled and said 'sorry about that' to me and completed the job. My point? She was on automatic pilot. She did not give a moment's thought to the decisions she made and I am sure they have not entered her head since.

That lady does it on the checkout. I do it on the phone when I am only half listening to someone and making notes or watching television at the same time. The person on a diet is magically unable to notice the biscuit they are eating. But how much more alive would we feel if we chose to be more aware of what we are doing? It is when we are making conscious choices that we feel most involved in our life and that is good for our performance and our self-esteem.

Each day at work, you have the opportunity to make many decisions – big ones or small ones. It doesn't matter. But many times, we just choose not to think about what we are doing. How often have you heard yourself say 'I don't want to think about that right now'? What effect does that have? The problem does not go away.

It niggles away at you. To feel fully alive think about the issue and deal with it. It feels a lot better.

We can never be conscious of everything. Now you are not conscious of your heartbeat or breathing. But you can be, and probably the last sentence made you think about them. But we can choose to think more about the many day-to-day interactions we have with people.

Do you actively think about your customers' needs or do you just go through a routine? Are you consciously listening to what they say, or just keeping an ear out for what you want to hear? What you say to people matters, so a moment's thought may improve the communication.

If you think about how you do these things, it does another important thing. It makes you more open to changing what you do and being more successful. You may have to face up to being wrong about things at times, but that becomes the opportunity for doing things a new way. What you may find is that your understanding of yourself and your customers increases.

The most flexible people are the ones that will survive best in a rapidly changing world of work. They are the ones that are doing more thinking about what it is they are doing, what effect it is having, and being consciously open to trying something new if that works better.

For them, being aware has been a habit. On Monday jot down the number of times you become aware when previously you would have operated on automatic. Not just at work. You will find that you are missing a lot during your 16 hours!

Quality of life

We hear a lot of talk about quality of life and it is one of those notoriously difficult concepts to define. You know it when you see it. You know it when you feel it. But because one person's heaven is another person's hell, it is difficult to produce a checklist that you can use to rate how good your life is.

When we are dealing with illness, or with the declining powers of the elderly, we can immediately see how their range of choices about how life is lived is narrowing. But for those of us who are fortunate to be in the whole of our health the path to maximising quality of life is not clear.

I was listening to *Sunday Miscellany* in the beautiful Thomastown countryside and was struck by one woman's story of how she changed her life. Like many people, she was under the constant pressure of juggling the demands of work and two children and they felt like demands. One morning her youngest son was clearly not feeling great and this threatened to mess up her schedule. There simply was not time to arrange for someone to look after him and still get to work on time so he got dressed for school. Then in one of those moments that change lives she suddenly decided to put him back to bed and take the day off work. What was unthinkable a quarter of an hour earlier became the obvious thing to do. She continued to take time off work until he was well again and this led to her reorganising her life and finances and quitting work to be able to care for her children. As she reached the end of her story and described collecting her son from school and the smile on his face you could hear the smile in her voice. Life had ceased to be going through the motions and had turned into a quality article. Quality of life, it seems to me, is reflected in the beam on your face. If you don't feel it there, then it is time to review your options.

What struck me about this woman's story, apart from her obvious happiness about the outcome, was the random way her defining moment happened. A less worrying illness, a different day of the week, a nearby relative, the cleaner coming, or any one of a number of 'solutions' that day and the outcome might have been different. We are creatures of habit and routine and it is difficult to step back and take a good look at how we are spending our time.

Our abilities and opportunities enable us to make choices. The choices for most of us are far from limitless. You have to decide to go to the restaurant or buy that coat. You cannot afford both – if you must have both, something else has to go, or some more work has to be done. There are decisions to be made, but usually when you take a good look at your life there is more room for manoeuvre than you might have imagined.

The beginning of the process is to make two lists. On the left-hand side of the page write down the things that you do not like doing, that bring you down, that you would happily never do again if it were possible. Some of the things on that list will stay there no matter what as that is just the nature of life. We have to do things that we would rather not do. But there may be many things on that list that could be approached a different way if you were a bit more flexible about it.

The second column is for all the things that you genuinely enjoy doing and would like to do more of. Everything on this list should pass the 'beam on your face' test. So whether it is spending one night a week on your own with the phone off the hook or climbing a mountain, visiting your aunt in the country or going to the pictures, there are going to be things on that list that are do-able if you make the decision to do them.

They may not be as life encompassing as the woman on the radio. Or they may put her in the shade. She was ready to stop work and had been shutting out the hankering. Listen to the hankering part of your mind. Is there anything there that is giving you a nudge towards putting the smile back on your face more often?

Jobless – but gainfully employed

'There you are writing about work and you can hardly remember what it was like to have a job'.

The point was put to me jocularly, over a glass of wine, but it set me thinking. Well, it is true. Jobless, but thankfully usually gainfully employed. In a varied worklife that began with petrol stations and factories as a student, had I learned anything along the way?

'This above all. To thine own self be true'. It takes about half a life-time to understand the wisdom in that.

In my worklife, the notion of career changed beyond recognition, unemployment and emigration went from sucking the life out of the country to becoming memories of the bad times. Jobs became contracts. Pensions became portable. We went from not being able to have a phone to losing a third of our money fondly thinking we could own the company. Our whole conception of work, money, and what we expect out of life changed at a pace never before seen.

I have been working since 1978 and I left my only permanent and pensionable job, lecturing in Trinity College, in 1984. My mother at the time thought I was mad … leaving that job for a short-term contract in RTE producing television programmes! In truth, she had always liked the status of TCD whereas she could take or leave RTE. I always regret that she died before I did my stint with the *Late Late Show*. That would have made her proud.

My father began working in insurance at 18 and retired from the same company 46 years later. That is my idea of hell, and I think it was his for the final decade or so. With the arrogance of youth, I assumed the good life would come my way as my entitlement.

I never planned anything. That is partly my fault, partly my parents' fault, and largely my school's fault. So, I stumbled into Trinity to study physics and maths because I was 'good at them' and one bewildered term later discovered psychology and switched courses.

I did psychology without any notion of how I would ever earn a living at it. So, what does one do in that situation? Research, a

PhD, and lecture … an extended education and some of the most pleasurable times of my life were when my passion was psychology and I could be paid for teaching it.

But the media bug bit and I realised I was not cut out to be an academic. To play the publication game you need to be single-minded, which I am not. Or you need to be so brilliant that you can indulge your interests and still research and publish and I was a lower breed of animal.

Did I learn anything? As an academic, I think I learned a lot about a little, and remained disturbingly ignorant of the country I lived in. That was thankfully rectified during my decade in RTE. There is probably no group of people in Ireland who know more about this country, its history, its people and every highway and by-way than the producers, reporters and camera crews in RTE. It was a truly pleasurable time. I learned the value of this medium being enmeshed in its culture. I left RTE in 1996.

I was in my forties, an interesting time in life when you first fully comprehend that your time on this planet is limited. Life it not a rehearsal. It was well put by Bono recently in a marvellous song, 'Kite' …*I'm not afraid to die, I'm not afraid to live, and when I'm flat on my back, I hope I'll feel that I did'*.

So one dusts oneself off and moves on. Today I never know what the future holds beyond a few months or sometimes weeks. But thankfully, the self-belief, always a transient thing when you are only as good as your last job, is intact. I look back over the diary and see projects with the likes of Gay Byrne, Mary Kennedy, Brendan O'Carroll, Marty Whelan, Ronnie Drew, Eleanor Shanley and Neven Maguire. Now that is a talented bunch and who wouldn't be thankful for those opportunities? Then there were the joys and rigours of *Treasure Island* and its fabulous crew.

What began with a phone call became a regular and fulfilling relationship with the *Sunday Independent*. Out of other friendships came the opportunity to join the team who pitched successfully for the local radio licence in Carlow and Kilkenny. It is with a sense of pride that I own a small chunk of the radio station in the town I grew up in and I know my parents would have been enormously proud.

I find myself returning to psychology. Life turns full circle and I'm doing a little planning this time! The youth that so despised the rat race now knows just how seductive it can be.

If we are going to spend the best years of our life working, it had better be worthwhile and enjoyable. Thankfully it is. There are so many challenges out there to look forward to. But I feel a tinge of relief that my mother is no longer with us. She would never have got a night's sleep!

QUICK THINKING ON YOUR FEET

Valerie Pierce

Success, both in business and in everyday life, depends on clear and effective thinking – especially under pressure. Whatever your purpose, how you think about it will determine your success. *Quick Thinking on your Feet* will show you how to strengthen your thinking techniques and so improve the quality and productivity of your work – you will be able to work smarter rather than harder.

LIFE AFTER LOSS

Christy Kenneally

What do you say after you've said 'Sorry for your trouble'? This is not just a book for the bereaved but for everyone who is unsure how to act and what to say when faced with friends, family, loved ones, colleagues and acquaintances who have been bereaved. *Life After Loss* was written for what the author calls the 'second circle' who are dealing with the bereavement of others. They include family, friends, colleagues, employers, carers, nurses, doctors, priests, pastors, social workers and counsellors. Drawing on twenty years of lecturing, training and broadcasting on the subject of bereavement, Christy Kenneally has put together a book filled with human interest, anecdote and even humour.